* * * * *

"Nuanced, smart, and compelling...this is an invaluable resource for both the non-monogamous and the curious."

—LUCAS F. WILSON, Ph.D., author of *Shame Sex Attraction* and postdoctoral fellow at the University of Toronto Mississauga

"With raw honesty and soulful depth, *Love Beyond Monogamy* doesn't treat polyamory as a trend or a debate to win, but as a radical path of connection, growth, and truth."

—REV. ELLE DOWD, activist and author of *Baptized in Tear Gas*

"*Love Beyond Monogamy* is the perfect book for queer folks who may be struggling with their religion, desire, and sexuality."

—ANDREW GURZA, author of *Notes From A Queer Cripple*

"For religious seekers looking to learn more about polyamory, polyamorous folks looking to explore religious traditions, and any others with an eye toward expanding beyond rigid frameworks of religion and romance—this book is a true gift."

—RABBI LEX ROFEBERG, senior Jewish educator of Judaism Unbound

"This book shows how pleasure, spirituality, and love...work beautifully together."

—KRISTIN KEEFE, LMHC (licensed mental health counselor)

"Whether you are exploring ethical non-monogamy or love someone who is, or you just want to deepen your own relationships, this book is a powerful and much-needed read."

—SHANNON T.L. KEARNS, author of *No One Taught Me How To Be A Man: What a Trans Man's Experience Reveals About Masculinity*

* * * * * *

* * * * * *

"Packed with wisdom for anyone willing to open their hearts, minds, and spirits to new possibilities for deeper relationship, interdependent liberation, and even divine intervention."

—REV. MICAH BUCEY, author of *The Book of Tiny Prayer*
and senior minister of Judson Memorial Church

"Regardless of your relational structure, *Love Beyond Monogamy* contains wisdom that will enhance your relationships. Brian has given us a gift in this book."

—MATTHIAS ROBERTS, therapist and author
of *Beyond Shame* and *Holy Runaways*

"Insightful and affirming, *Love Beyond Monogamy* weaves together modern psychology, polyamorous community wisdom, and the teachings of a wide range of faiths into an illuminating exploration of their resonance and shared values."

—RYAN G. WITHERSPOON, Ph.D., clinical psychologist

"A great resource for those looking to explore or better understand how to find and create spiritual practices and belief structures for those who are sometimes pushed to the margins."

—DR. LIZ POWELL, author of *Building Open Relationships*

"For those of us who grew up being told there is only one right way to have a body and only one right way to love, this book is a healing balm and a compassionate challenge to revisit our assumptions about relationships and forge the life we actually want to live."

—EMILY JOY ALLISON, author of *#ChurchToo: How Purity
Culture Upholds Abuse and How to Find Healing*

* * * * * *

Love Beyond Monogamy

How Polyamory Can Enrich Your Spirituality, Faith, and Relationships

BRIAN G. MURPHY

Jessica Kingsley Publishers
London and Philadelphia

First published in Great Britain in 2026 by Jessica Kingsley Publishers
An imprint of John Murray Press

1

Copyright © Brian G. Murphy 2026

A CIP catalogue record for this title is available from the
British Library and the Library of Congress

ISBN 978 1 80501 3 631
eISBN 978 1 80501 3 648

Printed and bound in the United States by Integrated Books International

Jessica Kingsley Publishers' policy is to use papers that are natural,
renewable and recyclable products and made from wood grown in
sustainable forests. The logging and manufacturing processes are expected
to conform to the environmental regulations of the country of origin.

Jessica Kingsley Publishers
Carmelite House
50 Victoria Embankment
London EC4Y 0DZ

www.jkp.com

John Murray Press
Part of Hodder & Stoughton Limited
An Hachette UK Company

The authorised representative in the EEA is Hachette Ireland,
8 Castlecourt Centre, Dublin 15, D15 XTP3, Ireland (email: info@hbgi.ie)

Contents

Acknowledgments

This book could not exist if I was not blessed by a sprawling network of family and friends who model together every day what love beyond monogamy can look like, and who have believed in, championed, and supported my work over the years.

To my chosen family and families of origin, for forming me into the person I am. To Matt, for your unwavering friendship, the way you sharpen me to be the best version of myself, for the way you model love and commitment to everyone around you, and for your ability to make me laugh until it hurts. To my husband Peter, thank you for growing with me over nearly half a lifetime, for loving every version of me, and for believing in me and in us, even when I have doubts. Thank you for listening to me try to make sense of what this book could be and trusting me to tell parts of our story. To our queer family—Sam, Josh, Brian, Peter, Chris, and Matt—I love you boys more than words can express. It sometimes felt as if I was cheating writing this book because I channeled so much of your wisdom into it. To Brianna, you know me inside and out, and help me see clearly what I might otherwise miss. To my mom, who has been helping me write well and inspiring me to help others for as long as I can remember. To my dad, who has been a constant cheerleader as I tackled this first book.

To Shannon T.L. Kearns, for being my creative partner and one of my best friends. Thank you for seeing the wisdom of polyamory as a monogamous person, pushing me to share it more, and for helping me to become a better writer, scholar, and friend.

To Asher, my first postal service business partner, for your love, support, encouragement, and insight, proving that friendship can transcend city limits. And to Micah, my first creative collaborator, for stoking the fire of not settling for the way things are and having the courage to do something about it.

To Haven, for bringing faith and sexuality together in an integrated way for me, for modeling a soulful and unflinching pursuit of justice, and for helping me to tell my story publicly for the first time. I can trace every story I've ever told back to that conference room in Seattle.

To Jonathan V and Jonathan M, for lending your professional therapeutic wisdom to my work both in front of and behind the scenes, and for your encouragement when imposter syndrome was raging strong.

To all the friends with whom I've rambled on about polyamory for hours on end, the insights from those conversations are some of the bedrocks of this book. Especially to Charlie, David H, Jonathan C, and Hunter.

To Casey, for believing in me and Peter from the very beginning and for being my first model of a queer chosen family. The community you brought together in Brooklyn all those years ago changed my life.

To the Sanctuary Collective community and especially to all the alumni of our polyamory and spirituality cohorts, for showing up as your authentic selves, modeling for us all that polyamory and faith are already thriving in the world; and for your feedback on the ideas and early excerpts from this book.

To my agent Trinity McFadden, for taking a chance on me and this book and working tirelessly to find it the right home. You saw the vision for what this could be from our first meeting and I've trusted you ever since.

To my editors: Alex, for believing in this book, and Jane, for getting it across the finish line.

To all the prophets and priests of the queer and polyamorous community, thank you for paving the way for me. In particular, this book could not be what it is without the incredible bodies of work produced by Jase, Emily, and Dedeker of *Multiamory*, Cunning Minx of *Poly Weekly*, Kevin Patterson of *Poly Role Models*, and Dossie Easton and Janet Hardy, authors of *The Ethical Slut*.

And to everyone I've loved, in all the ways that we can love, thank you for leaving smudges of yourself all over me and in turn all over this book.

Introduction

The act of welcoming a stranger into your midst is considered an act of sacred hospitality in all the major world religions. Buddhism, Hinduism, Judaism, Christianity, and Islam all understand hospitality to be not just a good deed, but an obligation.

But what does welcoming a stranger into your bedroom have to teach us about hospitality?

Most religious and spiritual paths also speak to an abundance of God's love for us. This is true of traditional monotheistic faiths as well as pop spirituality. Turn to just about any article or podcast on finances or business, and you'll find secular leaders speaking to secular audiences about an "abundance mindset." Popularized by Stephen R. Covey in his book *The 7 Habits of Highly Effective People*,[1] which has sold over 40 million copies, an abundance mindset is the belief that there is more than enough resources, joy, money, and success to share with everyone.

But do we really believe in abundance? Scarcity might color your experiences of both faith and relationships more than you realize. Thankfully, insights from polyamory help everyone—whatever your relationship structure or spiritual inclination—to experience abundance more fully in all areas of our lives.

I'm the co-founder and director of spiritual practices for QueerTheology.com, an education platform and online community to help lesbian, gay, bisexual, transgender, queer and questioning (LGBTQ+) people heal from spiritual shame, integrate their sexualities, genders, and spirituality, and develop healthy practices that bring them into alignment with their deepest values, whether inside or outside traditional religious spaces. Over the course of ten-plus years, we've produced more than 500 podcast episodes, worked with over 1,000 clients, and reached over three million people in 200 countries. Our books, articles, and videos have been used in college curricula, professional development courses for therapists, and Bible studies and sermons in churches around the world. I also have a private relationship coaching practice, focusing on clients who are in or are interested in open or polyamorous relationships.

I came to this work because the support and resources I was looking for didn't exist yet. At the time my creative partner Fr. Shannon T.L. Kearns and I started QueerTheology.com, the conversation about "LGBTQ+ issues" and spirituality was firmly centered around debating whether it was even okay to be LGBTQ+ and a person of faith. A central pillar of the case for LGBTQ+ acceptance was that queer people could—and should—be monogamous. A sex-positive, polyamory-inclusive vision for faith was nowhere to be found. I also found that queer male voices were, surprisingly, absent from the most popular polyamory books, conferences, and resources. There was an acknowledgment that many queer men have a long history of embracing non-monogamy, but it often felt as if queer men were being talked *about* rather than talked *with* and that our promiscuity and open relationships were somehow separate from polyamory.

While my personal relationships and professional practice have been enriched by the wisdom of polyamorous authors and educators, many of whom I talk about in this book, I also speak and work from my own personal perspective. I came out as queer (first as gay, later as bisexual) at 18. I started dating my now-husband Peter at 23 and we opened up our relationship just 18 months into what is now a more than 15-year relationship. On the one hand, I embrace a non-hierarchical, anything-is-on-the-table version of polyamory. I have had other significant relationships we hoped would last a lifetime, we've been long-distance multiple times over the course of our 15-year relationship, and we don't even have dedicated sides of the bed. On the other hand, Peter and I have been together since we were 23 and are now legally married. When we considered legal marriage and a wedding-esque celebration, we approached them as two distinct decisions. Legal marriage was a practical consideration on how we can best care for each other right now. We agreed that could change in the future if circumstances changed—such as wanting to include other friends or partners in a legally equal caretaking arrangement. Our social and spiritual wedding was a decision that we have something special worth celebrating, and was crafted to celebrate not just us as a couple but the sprawling communities and chosen families that have shaped and sustained us. A rabbi and two close Jewish friends signed our *ketubah*, our best friend and our two oldest friends since childhood signed our New York State marriage license.

Separating the legal marriage from the communal celebration is, of course, available to anyone (and I invite everyone to consider it for themselves) but I don't know that I would have thought to do that without the influence of polyamory and queerness in my life—both of which taught me to question assumptions, define relationships on my own terms, and chart my own path. It was friends who were queer women who modeled a positive, queer, communal vision of polyamory for me—a way of relating that made me think "I could do that too." I have been polyamorous almost as long as I have openly identified as queer. For me, polyamory, queerness, and promiscuity are intertwined.

My queer and polyamorous identities are also shaped by experiences of activism and community organizing in New York City. My roommate Casey would host an annual Passover seder with the queer *haggadah* her roommates wrote and that she and her partner adapted to be even more social-justice focused. Each year, we'd squeeze a dozen or so queers—some Jewish, some not—into our tiny Brooklyn apartment. And every year, Casey's mother and grandmother would attend. It was a vision of the way the world could be. My friends and I organized for racial and LGBTQ+ justice in New York City and beyond through organizations and events like Queers for Economic Justice, the Audre-Lorde Project, Soulforce, Trans Day of Action, and the Philadelphia Transgender Health Conference. In my twenties, I co-founded a small, grassroots project to support LGBTQ+ students who were organizing on Christian college campuses. We recruited friends, pastors, teachers, poets, parents, and community organizers to serve as mentors. I received training through GLAAD (an LGBTQ+ media advocacy non-profit organization), worked with GLSEN (an non-profit organization focused on supporting LGBTQ+ students in K–12 education), organized with the Human Rights Campaign, and even met with the Holy See's representative to the United Nations—a Roman Catholic cardinal who reported directly to the Pope!

While I grew up attending an evangelical Presbyterian church, I also attended diverse, multicultural public schools. Close to half of my friends were Jewish, with a smattering who were Muslim or Hindu, and even a few crunchy secular humanists. At home, my parents encouraged critical thinking and religious pluralism and my mom proudly identified as liberal, pro-choice, and a feminist. When I was 19, my mom asked if I was going to convert to Judaism. I answered "No!" as quickly and as instinctively as when she asked me if I was gay as a teenager. As it turns out, she was on to something both times: I officially converted to Judaism in 2023. There is a version of my story where I grew up steeped in conversative Christian culture, with parents who met on the way to YoungLife camp and whose friends were mostly evangelical Christians. I was active in youth group, went on to study religion in college, and later founded the first explicitly *queer* Christian podcast and online community. There's another version of the story where I grew up active in high school theater, with best friends who were mostly Jewish, being able to recite many Jewish blessings from heart because I'd picked them up by osmosis at more b'nei mitzvahs than I can count. There's a version of my story where my partner and I have been open for the vast majority of our relationship, where we work to break down hierarchies in all of our relationships and hold space for each to take whatever form is right for it, where we've each had other serious relationships and entanglements, where we've lived long-distance, and where casual, sometimes even anonymous, sex is the norm. In that version, we have the most non-traditional relationship of any of our friends. There's also a version of the story where we've been together since just after college, where we are each other's first serious relationship, where we are legally married. In this version of the story, we have the most traditional relationship of any of our friends.

All those versions of my story are true. There may be a version of your story that you are most widely known for, maybe it's even the version of your story that you believe most about yourself, but I'd venture to guess it isn't the only version of your story. Like Walt Whitman, you contain multitudes! Both queerness and polyamory call us to question assumptions and blur boundaries (themes we'll explore in greater detail later in this book). As you read through this book, I invite you to pay attention to all the different versions of yourself, even (especially!) the ones that seem to contradict one another. In the Talmud, there are two main schools of thought: the House of Shammai and the House of Hillel. On many important points of Jewish law and custom, they disagree. In almost all cases, Hillel's argument is the one that is ultimately accepted as binding.

Yet both perspectives are recorded. Jewish tradition teaches that there is value, wisdom even, in understanding both perspectives and that one day in the future the decisions may be flipped on their head and we will follow the tradition of Beit Shammai. Pay attention to your inner "Beit Shammai" or as Robert Frost says, your "road not taken." There is wisdom there, too.

In my work as a relationship coach and spiritual educator, I sit at the intersection of two spheres of life that many modern adults have been taught to think of as entirely separate. But my work as a sex and spirituality educator shows that they are actually deeply intertwined. In my relationship coaching practice, I work predominantly with LGBTQ+ people, some of whom grew up with backgrounds as far-ranging as evangelical Christian, nominally Methodist, Orthodox Jewish, or observantly Muslim. Despite casting their religious practices aside, many still experience shame in their bodies, sexualities, and desires. They don't necessarily want to be religious in any traditional sense of the word, but they do want to heal from the harm that religion has caused them and the lingering effects it has on their bodies and spirits.

As the director of Spiritual Practices for QueerTheology.com, I work predominantly with people who identify as religious—some of whom were raised religious, others who came to religion or changed religions as adults—and who desperately *want* their faith to be a central part of their lives but who feel a deep alienation from their sexual selves.

What I have found is that whether you are religious, spiritual-but-not-religious, or completely secular, or whether you are Christian, Jewish, Buddhist, Hindu, atheist, still undecided, or something else entirely, the merging of sex and spirit transforms both and has the explosive potential to enrich not just your own life but also your family, friends, and community.

This book has two audiences in mind. I write for the monogamous person of faith or spiritual seeker. We stand on the precipice of another sexual revolution. In a 2020 study of 822 currently monogamous people by Kinsey Institute research fellow Justin Lehmiller, nearly one-third said that having an open relationship was their favorite sexual fantasy, and 80 percent wanted to act on it.[2] Perhaps you yourself haven't got that far, but you've felt hemmed in by the traditional relationship expectations placed on you by society. Or perhaps one of the one in five adults who have been in an open or polyamorous relationship is in your family, your friend group, or your spiritual community and you want to understand and support them better. More than that, though, I write this book for you because polyamory can offer new insights into faith that will enrich *your* spirituality, and new helpful practices for relationships that can improve *your* monogamous relationship. The models of polyamory can also help you release religious baggage and claim a spiritual practice that fits *you*.

I write also for the sex-positive and possibly polyamorous person who has been alienated from traditional spirituality and yet longs for a deeper, more intimate connection with That Which Is Bigger Than Ourselves. We do so much intellectual work to sort out the complexities of our sexuality, our shame, and our relationship structures, and then to advocate for a more just world for ourselves and for others; how can we be comforted, healed, soothed, refreshed, and inspired?

If you're looking for practices to nourish your inner life and support your outer life in a way that (re)connects you to yourself, to the people important to you, and to your deepest values, this book is for you.

As we move through this book, we'll look at key spiritual and relational concepts like love, commitment, ritual, worship, and even God (you can peek at the table of contents for a preview of where we're going and skip around to where your curiosity takes you). In each chapter, I'll outline how polyamory gives new insights to this element of the sacred, as well as how the sacred and sex can be fused together to create something that is greater than the sum of its parts.

I said I write for two audiences, but that's not quite true. One of the things that queerness and polyamory both embrace is a blurring of binaries. The distinction between friend and lover is not always so clear. This blurring of binaries is present in many religions, too. In Christianity, the very existence of Jesus blurs the distinction between divine and human. Daily blessings in Judaism, *brachot*, transform the mundane into the sacred: there is even a blessing to say after you go to the bathroom, marveling at the wonder and complexity of our human bodies. So while I say this book has two audiences, there is a good chance that you are already a mix of two.

In my work as a relationship coach, I've listened to non-religious clients use quite religious language to talk about their sexual activities and desires. In my work as a spiritual educator, I've seen cisgender, heterosexual, monogamously married people have an innate sense that sex can be *good*, and that they aren't being served by keeping sex and spirit separate.

In this book, you'll learn to blur the boundaries between sex and spirit, between body and soul, and perhaps most importantly between "The One and Only" and "everyone else." It's my hope that by the end of this book, your relationships with yourself, your partner or partners, the people in your life, and your higher power, however you understand that, are more integrated than ever. From that place of integration, you will be able to approach both sex and spirituality with more ease and greater passion.

Let's get started.

CHAPTER 1

We Have Always Had Many Loves

"The Bible is clear" is a phrase that has been used against oppressed and marginalized people for as long as there has been a canonical Christian Bible. The blood libel of Jews, the justification of slavery, the evils of non-marital sexual intimacy, and of course LGBTQ+ lives, loves, and bodies, are just a few notable examples. Regressive Christians trot out "The Bible is clear" to justify their manipulative and controlling theological and policy positions; but well-meaning progressive Christians, and even secular activists, unwittingly reinforce the false notion of a biblical, or even traditional, definition of marriage and family.

The campaign for marriage equality for same-gender couples was built largely on the back of talking points which asserted that "loving, committed, monogamous same-gender couples" should have equal rights as their heterosexual (or hetero-seeming) counterparts. The stated message is that LGBTQ+ relationships are "normal" and "traditional;" the implied message is that "normal" and "traditional" relationships are stable, long-lasting, and monogamous. But is that even true?

Adam and Eve have a lot of explaining to do. The first biblical couple has become an archetypal model for how many of us in modernity think about marriage. While the Bible shouldn't be used as a guidebook for public policy (or even universal morality, I'd argue), there are 1.9 billion Muslims, 2.4 billion Christians, and 15 million Jews who claim Adam and Eve as part of their sacred story. The biblical narrative is sparse on details when it comes to the first couple. In fact, there is no indication in the text that they had a *wedding* in either a modern or ancient sense, only that the woman was the man's wife. None of the trappings of the institution of marriage had been developed yet; in this story, they are just two people alone in the world. The reason for this pairing is stated explicitly: "It is not good for the Human to be alone; I will make a fitting counterpart for him" (*The Contemporary Torah, JPS, 2007*, Genesis 2:18). Human relationships exist because it is not good for us to be alone—not to fulfill the institution of marriage.

Many of us—even many people in open or polyamorous relationships—take for granted that relationships *normally* are or *should be* stable, long-term, and monogamous; but the data just doesn't back that up. At best estimate, 45 percent of marriages end in divorce. Before couples even walk down the aisle, each partner has had, on average, eight other relationships prior.[3] On top of that, one quarter of married men and 15 percent of married women have had an affair.[4] And then, of course, not all relationships attempt or pretend to be monogamous.

When we talk about humans and monogamy, it's important to be clear about what we mean. Almost every single person in a monogamous marriage has already fallen in love with more than one person; eight, if the statistics are accurate. Between previous relationships, unethical affairs in ostensibly monogamous marriages, and a divorce rate on par with a coin toss, "one and only for forever and ever," is, in most cases, not just one, and just as likely forever as not.

In the middle school youth group at my church, I was taught that sex is like sticky tape. Every time you have sex with someone, you slap a big piece of your tape across them. Then, when that relationship eventually ends, you have to rip the tape off. It's now covered in the lint of their clothes. When a girl ripped her tape off of you, it would hurt. She would pull up hair and skin in the process. I was presumed to be a boy and so anyone I might one day have sex with was assumed to be a girl. Queer sex was hardly ever mentioned. I can remember only one passing reference to homosexuality at church from my entire childhood.

Metaphors like the tape one varied; yet in my work with queer and polyamorous people of faith on every inhabited continent, the shaming metaphors for sex at church are surprisingly consistent. There's the one where you start out with a beautiful rose (*you* are the beautiful rose, to be clear) and then pass it around the room. When each youngster is passed the rose, they pluck off a petal. By the time it makes it back to you, you're nothing but a battered and bare stalk. There's one where you start off with a delicious cookie (again, *you* are the delicious cookie). It's warm in your hand. You pass it to the person next to you. They take a bite, then another, savoring the doughy mix of sugar and chocolate. Then, before swallowing, they spit it back on the plate and pass it to the next person. Who would ever want a chewed-up cookie? It's not so delicious anymore, is it?! Depending on how cruel the church leader is, the point is satisfactorily made when the mushed-up cookies come rolling out of the first mouth. I've worked with clients who were forced to eat their friends' chewed-up cookie chunks.

These object lessons are, rightfully, appalling. Toxic messages about sex aren't contained to religion either. Mainstream secular straight dating culture is fixated on "body count," the number of sexual partners a person has had. It's an impossible standard to live up to—especially for women, who are judged both for having and not having sex. Whether you are queer or straight, monogamous or polyamorous, there is a good chance you've been made to feel shame about the sex you are—or are not—having. Sex doesn't tarnish you, or chew you up, or diminish the stickiness of your love and devotion, though. No. Your body is good. Your love is abundant. Your sex doesn't become less effective, meaningful, or valuable each time you share it. Quite the opposite, in fact! Sex and love, when shared, can multiply. Conversely, you aren't frigid or broken if you haven't had much or any sex. The way we talk about sex matters and we need better metaphors. The wisdom of polyamory reminds us that we *are* transformed by relationships and connections of all kinds; it's just that the transformation can be positive, holy even, if we remember to look for the sacred mixed up in our sexual and romantic connections.

I dated my first-ever boyfriend for three months, over two decades ago. Half a lifetime ago, I spent 0.69 percent of my life thus far in that relationship. And we were teenagers living in suburban Maryland, so we were probably *actually* together only a tenth of that time. If I tried, I could probably count the hours. Still, all these years later, I remember him fondly often. There is, in fact, no way that I could ever count the hours. Through text exchanges throughout the day, afternoon walks around our neighborhood park with our dogs, dinner dates and double dates, and sleepy phone calls well into the evening, we created a whole eternity out of just a dozen weeks.

Jason Silva talks about "inter-subjective ecstasy," the primal human urges for communication and connection, to be seen and understood. When we give each other pet names, spend a morning cuddled up under the sheets, take photos of every precious moment on a vacation, Silva says, "We are trying to find escapes from the despair. Together, we are creating a shared universe...Where we can *not* die." In those moments, the bliss of love causes time to stretch and even stop. We exist outside time for a moment.[5] Alan Harrington says, "Our lovers act as stand-ins in a stage-managed resurrection where the pilgrim without faith can die and live again."[6]

My first boyfriend and I only ever kissed, and we only dated for a few months, but he left me transformed. I can't help but carry him around with me wherever I go. There are bits and pieces of him that worked their way into my essence and changed who I am, how I see myself, and how I move through the world. I became more confident, more open-hearted, more "sticky" as a result of dating him, not less. Before him, I had mostly come to terms with my queerness and decided it was probably not a sin, but that was a tentative intellectual conclusion. The first time we held hands, I knew it was okay—no, that it was *good*—in the depths of my being. We were sitting next to each other on the floor of a friend's basement watching the season premiere of *Degrassi: The Next Generation*, the view of our hands blocked by a friend lounging in front of us. His fingers walked along the floor closer to mine, and my fingers sidled up next to his in return. Tentatively, they touched. Then intertwined. The assurance that *this is holy* jumped from his hand to mine just as surely as the slight static shock. I can still step back into that moment all these years later; it exists outside time. In that moment, I was reborn.

Every partner I've ever had has left a piece of themselves behind. The good, the bad, the beautiful, and the messy. Whether you are monogamous, polyamorous, something in between, or something else entirely, your life is almost certainly marked by many loves. The word polyamory comes from a Greek and a Latin root: *poly*, meaning many, and *amory*, meaning love. In the most literal definition of the word, everyone is polyamorous. We all have many loves. Whether or not you identify as polyamorous largely rests on how and when you count those loves. I've been with my husband Peter for 15 years now, but I dated a few other guys before him—and a few since we've been together. I loved many, if not all, of them. I still love them, in a way. Who do you love? Who have you loved? They are part of you too.

A person in a monogamous relationship hopefully loves their partner, but they probably also love their parents, kids from previous relationships, siblings, and even best friends. When I was six, my parents told me they were considering having another kid and asked what I thought.

"Yes, please!" I responded. "I'd like a sister!"

My parents chuckled and told me we'd have to wait to see whether it would be a sister. It didn't cross my mind for one second that my parents' interest in having a second child meant anything about their love for me. A potential new sister was a source of excitement. Having a sibling *did* change the relationship I had with my parents, though. Sometimes they had to leave me to take care of her. Sometimes my sister and I had activities on the same night, so only one parent could come to each. When my mom or dad traveled for work, I necessarily got less attention from the parent who was at home with us. That's just how families and parenting work. We take for granted that parents will have multiple kids. No one thinks that a parent's love is divided in two when the second child is born. Love can multiply when new love is added into the mix. I got a sister to love and to love me in return! Well into our adult lives, we still sign birthday and holiday cards to each other with "BF4L"—best friends for life.

There are many ways that we have many loves. Seventy-eight percent of mothers have more than one child, and 40 percent of American families are blended, with at least one partner having a child from a previous relationship before marriage.[7] Our ability to have many loves goes beyond traditional notions of marriage and family. In her popular sitcom The *Mindy Project*, Mindy Kaling declared, "A best friend isn't a person...it's a tier!" I have at least three people in my life whom I would call "my best friend," not counting my sister, partners, or parents. Films such as *Girls Trip* and *Bridesmaids* showcase the central role that friendship—deep, loving, vulnerable friendship—plays in our lives. That, too, is love. A century of romance novels, love songs, and romance movies have narrowly confined "love" to the sphere of romance, and defined it as a monogamous *a priori*. The lived reality of our lives is, of course, much more nuanced than that. Whether you are monogamous or polyamorous, you already have many loves.

It is important to note that non-monogamy is more common than you might imagine. According to a 2016 student in the *Journal of Sex & Marital Therapy*, about 20 percent of single United States adults reported that they had been in an ethically non-monogamous relationship.[8] A January 2020 YouGov poll[9] found that 32 percent of respondents said that their ideal relationship is non-monogamous to some degree, and among those in a relationship, 23 percent are non-monogamous to some degree.

It might be tempting to listen to the curbside preachers and televangelist pastors who decry "crumbling" families as a recent, moral failure, but the biblical record that so many of us are compared to (whether or not we believe in the Bible) is shockingly similar to (and in some cases more gruesome than) our present reality. At QueerTheology.com, I work with LGBTQ+ and polyamorous people of faith to reclaim, change, or leave their faith practice. We take "It is okay to be LGBTQ+ and a person of faith. It is okay to be polyamorous and a person of faith" as the starting point, rather than the finish line when it comes to the conversation of "LGBTQ+ and religion" or "polyamory and religion." For the first eight years of the *Queer Theology Podcast* (now the longest-running LGBTQ+ spirituality podcast), we journeyed through the Christian lectionary nearly three times. The lectionary is a three-year-long cycle that lays out four Bible passages every Sunday that many Christians and churches all read in sync. Through that exploration, we've uncovered a lot of different "biblical marriages."

If the story of Adam and Eve is taken literally (which, of course, it isn't meant to be), Adam marries his genetic twin. In this marriage, there isn't any wedding or marriage ceremony, no sacred ritual. They know each other, in the biblical sense, and that is that.

Abraham, considered to be the father of the world's "Abrahamic religions," including Judaism, Christianity, and Islam, had three wives.

In Genesis 16, while he was still married to Sarah, Abraham took on Hagar as a second wife. In this story, Abraham and Sarah had been unable to conceive a child, even after being promised by God that he would be "the father of many nations." Sarah was worried that perhaps she was infertile, and didn't want to stand in the way of Abraham having kids, so she suggested to Abraham that he marry Hagar as well.*

This story is not only a striking example of non-monogamy, but also a recognition that sometimes we cannot meet all of our partners' needs and desires. Together with Hagar, Abraham had his first son with his second wife: Ishmael. Fourteen years after Ishmael's birth, or so the story goes, Sarah gave birth to her first son: Isaac. In all relationships, monogamous or non-monogamous, sometimes the circumstances of the relationship we entered into changes. An unexpected child is born, a partner suffers an injury or a disease, a once-prosperous industry collapses and a spouse is left unemployed, a child or parent dies, a partner realizes later in life that they are queer, sex drives ebb and flow. We cannot know exactly the course our relationship will take when we enter into it. bell hooks wrote, "We cannot know love if we remain unable to surrender our attachment to power, if any feeling of vulnerability strikes terror in our hearts."[10] Stepping into the unknown is part of what it means to be in a deep, authentic relationship with another. Your partner may want to open—or close—your relationship. How can you love well through those vulnerable and uncertain times while remaining unattached to power? How do you stay open to change while true to yourself? The examples throughout this book, both ancient and modern, will give you some models to consider.

But first I want to pause here, to point out some of the many

---

*The Biblical account in Genesis describes Hagar as both a "concubine" and "wife" in different places.

problems in this Biblical story. The characters here are not role models we should emulate. The story of Abraham, Sarah, and Hagar is not a progressive, polyamorous one. Sarah "gives" Hagar to Abraham. However ancient listeners might have understood this story, we understand today that consent cannot be present when one partner has enslaved the other. So while the relationship between Abraham and Hagar is presented as a marriage, many modern readers rightfully see it as abuse and sexual violence. In Chapter 6, we'll look more at the importance of consent in all of our relationships. I share the story of Abraham, Sarah, and Hagar not as a model of an ethical relationship, but rather as a reminder that "biblical marriages" look lots of different ways. And maybe we shouldn't always take our cues from them!

Other famous biblical characters with multiple wives include Jacob (Abraham's grandson), Esau, Moses, King David, King Solomon, and Gideon. According to the account in 1 Kings, King Solomon was reported to have had "seven hundred wives, princesses, and three hundred concubines."

There are more ways than marriage to form meaningful sexual and romantic relationships. Song of Songs, a book in both the Christian and Jewish canons, is a celebration of pre-marital love and sexual intimacy. The couple speaks boldly and erotically of their passion for each other, sometimes directly and other times with sexually charged metaphors:

A bundle of myrrh is my well-beloved unto me; he shall lie all night betwixt my breasts.

I sat down under his shadow with great delight, and his fruit was sweet to my taste.

Awake, O north wind; and come, thou south; blow upon my garden, that the spices thereof may flow out. Let my beloved come into his garden, and eat his pleasant fruits.

Your stature is like a palm tree; your breasts are clusters of fruit. I said, "I will climb the palm tree and take hold of its fruit." May your breasts be like clusters of grapes, and the fragrance of your breath like apricots.

Let's go early to the vineyards; let's see if the vine has budded, if the blossom has opened, if the pomegranates are in bloom. There I will give you my love.

In the Bible, or this book of the Bible at least, sex isn't contained to marriage. It's not missionary-style, for-the-purposes-of-procreation-only. It's frenetic. It's self-directed. It's indulgent. It's swollen, hot, and juicy.

But that is not always the case. Elsewhere, in the Christian Bible, we find a much more tepid prescription for sexuality. In 1 Corinthians, Paul makes the case that the ideal status is single and celibate. Marriage is a last resort only. He says: "I'm telling those who are single and widows that it's good for them to stay single like me. But if they can't control themselves, they should get married, because it's better to marry than to burn with passion" (1 Corinthians 7:8–9, Common English Bible).

Whether it's sex between unmarried lovers, a non-monogamous marriage that would put modern polycules to shame with its scale and complexity, or an injunction against marriage altogether, "life-long monogamous marriage" is hardly the only biblical ideal.

In my undergraduate religious studies, I took a class called "Religion and Popular Culture in the United States." We looked at ways cultural traditions and institutions can take on spiritual, and even religious, meaning. Think about baseball games: they happen on a set schedule (like church/mosque/synagogue services); they are broken up into sections (like a liturgy); fans (congregants) join together to sing from a selection of standardized songs (like a hymnal); the players wear special outfits (like priestly robes) and so do the fans (like dressing up for service). A baseball game is more than a sport—it's a communal experience that brings us together with friends and strangers and expresses our values (such as loyalty, friendship, respect, competition, and excellence).

The United States of America, where I live, has developed a national religious system of its own. The Hebrew Bible has Adam, Noah, Abraham, and Moses as the founding patriarchs; the Christian faith counts Jesus, Peter, and Paul among its founders. The U.S. has its own patriarchs: George Washington, John Adams, Benjamin Franklin, Thomas Jefferson, and other founding fathers. We have prophets too, like Betsy Ross, Harriet Tubman, and Rev. Dr. Martin Luther King Jr. We have our own sacred texts: the Declaration of Independence, Constitution, and Bill of Rights. We have legislators, presidents, and judges who serve as priests, pastors, deacons, and elders. Many Americans say the Pledge of Allegiance and the National Anthem like Christians say the Lord's Prayer, Jews say the Shema, and Muslims pray *salat*.

"Official" religious texts are just one way that you might find and make meaning in your life. What stories, institutions, and traditions inform your life and values? The stories we see represented in movies, TV shows, and love songs teach us about the way relationships are "supposed" to look. Media normalizes intense jealousy, possessiveness, retribution, even violence as a way of enforcing a relationship. In the song "Before He Cheats," Carrie Underwood sings about destroying a lover's car over infidelity. In *Titanic*, the character Cal is jealous of Jack (played by Leonardo DiCaprio) and Jack's relationship with Cal's fiancé so Cal frames him for a crime and has him arrested. In the MTV reality show *Cheaters*, partners often get into fights when infidelity is caught on camera. In both fiction and reality, media often displays anger and violence as appropriate responses to infidelity. The central conflict in almost every story involving romance is the lead character choosing between one of two love interests. Bella chooses between Edward and Jacob in *Twilight*. Arthur chooses between Mikey and Ben in *Here's to Us*, Seth chooses between Summer and Anna in *The OC*, Amy chooses between Colin and Ephram in *Everwood*, Victor chooses between Benji and Rahim in *Love, Victor*, Katniss chooses between Peeta and Gale in *The Hunger Games*—the list could go on for pages. The message is clear: in romantic relationships, you must choose one, and only one, partner.

As we think about the types of relationships we want to form, it's important to inspect *why* we want them to take the structure we do. Where do those ideas come from? In modern storytelling, stories follow the same basic structure: inciting incident, conflict/rising action, climax, falling action, and resolution. "Will they? Won't they?" is an easy formula for conflict. The outcome is clear; the resolution is emotionally satisfying. There is a winner and a loser. It preys on our basest instincts.

Whether your sacred text is the Bible, *Star Trek*, both, or neither, it's important to take a close look at the messages you've internalized and then decide which are trustworthy and which you might reimagine or set aside entirely.

The Bible, much like the United States Constitution, proclaims some really beautiful messages, but both say some pretty terrible things as well. Whether we find ultimate meaning in a traditional sacred scripture, the laws of our land, the customs of our parents, the values of our friends, or some combination of therein, it's critical to recognize that there is more than meets the eye to "the way things have always been" and "what everyone is doing." The history and reality of love, relationships, and marriage is so much more complicated than pithy one-liners or the romantic ideals espoused in Hallmark movies.

The disconnect between the stories we were sold in romance novels, rom-coms, and well-meaning Sunday school sermons, and the reality of our lives and relationships has harmful consequences.

In 1999, I was a freshman in high school. One day in class, our teacher was indulging me and my friend Hannah as we chatted her up in an obvious attempt to avoid the assignment for the day. We found our way on to the topic of marriage and family, and my teacher shared with (a still very closeted) me that out of her seven siblings, all of whom had been married, the only two relationships to last were her gay brother and his partner and her younger sister who got pregnant at 16. (In 2020, 40 percent of births were to unwed mothers.[11]) The most "traditional"-seeming relationships can end in despair, while relationships that society looks down on as less valid can thrive. Be careful of whose standard you are holding yourself to.

The negative effects of this disconnect between ideal and reality go beyond physical and sexual consequences. In my work as a spiritual leader and relationship coach, nearly all of my clients have had some guilt or shame in the past about the state of their relationship, their body, their desires, their lack of relationship, or their relationship history. Far too many of them still carry that shame with them in the present.

In 2009, author and speaker Colin Wright threw a breakup party with his then-girlfriend.[12] They invited a bunch of their friends over to their shared apartment to celebrate their relationship and their friendship. There was music, there were stories, there were cocktails. And then, at midnight, they logged into Facebook and changed their relationship status to "single." Colin and his now-ex-girlfriend popped a bottle of champagne to the cheers of their friends. The party continued into the evening, and the next day Colin moved out of the country, starting a multi-year project called *Exile Lifestyle* in which he lived in a different country every three months. Breakups don't need to be failures. They don't need to be devastating. Your relationship doesn't need to be toxic, abusive, or terrible to end it. The decision to end it might be born out of recognizing the reality that you each want vastly different things, and you best fit into each other's lives in a different capacity. When a romantic relationship comes to an end, you can be thankful for the ways it changed you for good while releasing whatever wasn't serving you both.

Our relationships form and inform the very core of who we are as humans. Regardless of your religious views (or lack thereof), your closest relationships are in every meaningful way sacred. We can all recognize that, "it is not good for humans to be alone." One of the devastating effects of "the closet" is the way that it isolates LGBTQ+ people from healthy, deep, vulnerable relationships. Queer and poly-amorous people all know the experience of being shamed or silenced for who and how we love.

When I came out, many of my straight, cisgender friends asked me, "When did you know?" I can't point to a moment. Coming into the realization that I was queer was like embracing a new day at sunrise. At dawn, the world starts to light up even before the sun has peeked out above the horizon. When I was in fourth grade, a new boy moved to our town and started at my elementary school. I met David at my friend Patrick's birthday party. I was nine, but I can see scenes from that birthday party as surely as I can watch a movie. I remember crawling through the tunnels in the playground and bumping into David. I remember his smile. I remember his sparkling eyes and his adorable attached earlobes. I came home from that party and I remember telling my mom, "There's a new kid at school named David, and I want to be his friend." That's all it was. A new kid at school that I wanted to be my friend. There wasn't anything particularly queer about it. But with the distance of more than a few years, I can look back and wonder if those were some rays of light wrapping their way through the atmosphere and around the curvature of the earth, before the sun had peeked over the horizon.

David became one of my best friends, until he moved away after eighth grade—right around the time I was starting to put the dots together that the way I felt when I looked at the underwear models when shopping at Macy's with my parents could be connected to relationships I might actually have in real life.

I don't experience my polyamory as an orientation that is different from my friends and family in monogamous relationships. We all have complex webs of interpersonal relationships. This way works for me right now. Other ways work for other people. Opening up my relationship didn't feel like discovering a new aspect of my identity, but rather practicing with a new set of relationship skills. In my work as a relationship coach, some of my clients consider polyamory to be an innate orientation, but just as many are like me, who choose to practice polyamory or an open relationship because it aligns with their values and find that they can thrive in it.

Your relationships will be informed by your values and your understanding of that-which-is-bigger-than-yourself (what some folks call "God") and, in turn, those relationships can, if you will let them, inform your understanding of divinity. Whether you're delightfully single, are mending a broken heart, or are living in the day-to-day beauty and messiness of one or more romantic relationships, your experience of love and sex is a portal into the divine, just as much as, if not more so than, millennia-old scripture scrolls.

The spirit is already moving—it's time to tap into it.

CHAPTER 2

Reclaiming the Sacred

I f you looked around at the world and decided that religion is a destructive force in the world, you would have good reason and you would not be alone in thinking that. In the United States, white Christian nationalism is growing in visibility, fervor, and political power. The Iranian revolution in 1979 brought an end to an era of economic and social thriving in Iran and replaced it with a violent, authoritarian, and deeply sexist rule of law. Many Conservative Christians home-school their children to shelter their learning and are increasingly pushing their anti-science agenda in public school classrooms as well. Some ultra-Orthodox Jewish communities pressure their members to use "kosher phones"—smartphones retrofitted with censorship and monitoring software to only allow applications and websites approved by the group's leaders, while many evangelical Christians use similar "accountability software" to monitor their children's and friends' online browsing history. Which is to say nothing of religion's horrific historic track record: the Crusades, the Inquisition, the use of violence and imperialism to spread Christianity and Islam throughout the world, ethnic cleansing of the Rohingya people in Myanmar by the Buddhist majority, sectarianism and fundamentalism of all stripes which restricts knowledge, monitors communication, and foments distrust. And what about preachers holding "God Hates Fags" signs or, perhaps just as harmful, preachers who smile at you and tell you that who you love is sin? Why bother with the sacred at all?

"Life is bananas," says Kohenet* Avra Shapiro. "It's hard to be human in the world and especially in today's world. I find it to be incredibly grounding and also life-affirming and life-enhancing to take up practices that connect us with something bigger than ourselves." But why bother engaging in established, "traditional" faith traditions and spiritual practices? For Shapiro, "for better or worse, there is a kind of magic and a kind of rootedness that comes with working with something that is so old and making it your own." This rootedness extends in multiple directions: we are "vertically" connected through time to those who have come before us and those who will come after us, as well as "horizontally" connected across the world with those who are currently practicing in similar ways.[13] In addition to this magic and rootedness that can come from connecting with ancient traditions, there are present, practical concerns as well. Whether we like it or not, religion is a major influence throughout the world, and always has been. This is true on a personal level: our family's religious beliefs (and sometimes their reaction against their own religious experiences) shape our personal lives in deep and profound ways. It

---

*Kohenet is the feminine version of kohen, or priest, in Hebrew. The Kohanim ran the Temple in Jerusalem until its destruction in 70 CE. Today, a Kohen is a male-line descendant of those priests, and they are still given places of ceremonial honor in some congregations. Rabbi Jill Hammer and Taya Shere coined the term kohenet and founded the Kohenet Hebrew Priestess Institute in 2005. While the Institute closed in 2023, the website (https://kohenet.org) explains, "Reclaiming the title of 'kohenet' reminds us that the spiritual practices of women, gender-queer people, and others outside the religious authority structure matter to our past, present and future as much as the sages and teachings widely regarded as the core of Jewish culture."

is also true on structural levels: religion shapes culture and public policy, even in our modern era, and even in countries that are ostensibly secular. Puritanical Protestant Christianity is a driving force in the United States and Canada, while the Roman Catholic Church influences culture, policy, and even indigenous religious practices in Mexico and Central and South America. Islam is the official religion of 27 countries around the world[14] and that influence explicitly extends to law. In Israel, religious authorities oversee *all* marriages; there is no such thing as a secular marriage in Israel (though the government does recognize marriages between two partners, of any gender, religion, or no religion, performed elsewhere).

If you are reading this book, your life has been touched by religion in some way. Whether or not you remain "religious," in the sense of identifying with a specific religion and regularly engaging in its practices, is up to you. At QueerTheology.com, we put equal value on reclaiming your religious heritage, finding a new spiritual home that fits better, or leaving established faith all together. What is important is that you choose with intention; that you do the work to heal; that if you decide to stay, you make it your own; and if you decide to leave, you leave well. The importance of choosing with intentionality is also true for how you decide to structure your relationships, and many of the practices for intentionally choosing will be similar for both spheres of your life, as you'll see throughout this book.

"Human beings find themselves in quite the predicament. With our minds we have the capacity to ponder the infinite, seemingly capable of anything, yet we're housed in a heart-pumping, breath-gasping, decaying body," said author and cultural anthropologist Ernest Becker. "To have emerged from nothing; to have a name, consciousness of self, deep inner feeling; an excruciating yearning for life and self-expression. And with all this; yet to die."[15] This pull between the yearning for life and the knowledge of death is something all humans share. You do not need to be a Christian, Muslim, Hindu,

Jew, Buddhist, or anything else to be a religious person, to be in touch with the sacred: you simply need to be human. To be alive, is already to be sacred. Too many of us—especially our religious leaders—have lost sight of that fundamental truth. Too often, religion is used as a force for controlling, rather than liberating, our minds and bodies. In 1962, Robert Anton Wilson wrote for the Mattachette Review about the interplay between sexual freedom and government and social control:

> A governor, we can safely say, has less problems in enforcing obe-
> dience if his subjects are mystical, religious and frightened of sex.
> The reason for this is easy to understand. Sex denial is very close to
> being absolutely impossible, and—as the subtle Jesuits knew long
> before Freud—even when the would-be ascetic thinks he has "tri-
> umphed" over the flesh, it sneaks up on him from a new direction
> and takes him by surprise. Thus, the inevitable consequence of sex
> denial is guilt: that special guilt which comes of continual failure
> to accomplish that which you consider "good.".…A guilt- ridden man
> is an easy man to manipulate and force to your own will, because
> self-respect is the prerequisite of independence and rebellion, and
> the guilt-ridden person can have no self-respect.[16]

Claiming our sexual freedom is an important step in the process of claiming our whole freedom. And recognizing the source of many of the sex-negative messages we receive—fear and control—is an important step in befriending our bodies and desires again. As you read this book, you may notice what seems to be a glaring omission but which is actually a considered ethical and theological choice: this book does not seek to "make a case" for the ethics of non-monogamy by rebutting sex-negative and anti-polyamory perspectives. To do so would concede to a fundamental assumption: that a restrictive and mononormative worldview is the default while an expansive and polyamorous one requires defending. That would be an ahistorical position: various forms of non-monogamy have always existed in human cultures throughout time and around the world. History is full of civilizations where one form or another of non-monogamy is either widely present or the default. Today, despite lacking legal protections or mainstream cultural recognition in most countries, polyamorous people and relationships not only exist but are thriving. I will share some of those stories and insights, but I will not insult their dignity by turning them into a high-school debating club exercise. Rather than assume a defensive posture, which many non-monogamous people are already forced to do with friends, family, and in their religious communities, this book seeks to explore—and even "make a case for"—polyamory and other forms of non-monogamy on our own terms. It is my sincere hope that by the time you finish this book, such "what about" arguments will seem simple and reductive and that the goodness—the sacredness, even—of non-monogamous relationships will be clearly evident.

I spent years paralyzed by fear of my body and my desires. I worried there was this deeply unacceptable part of me and I didn't know what to do with it. I would tell myself that my desires were wrong. I would ignore them and suppress them. And eventually they would sneak up on me and I would snap. Most of my "relationships" in college started as drunken hookups. Those were the only times I could let my guard down enough to acknowledge and act on my desires. Jeremy was different. We met through a mutual friend. For our first proper date, we drove an hour from the University of Southern California's campus near downtown Los Angeles—where I was studying the seemingly unlikely combination of film production and religion—to go mini-golfing in Sherman Oaks. Jeremy was cute and we liked each other and we did cute, "innocent" things like hold hands and playfully hip-check each other to flirt. But I couldn't quite escape my shame.

After a month or so, an acquaintance that I knew through Campus Crusade for Christ died in a skateboarding accident. I fell into a shame spiral. Here was this young, good-looking man of God out there living his life for God, or so I imagined, and he just died. But at least he would be in heaven, I thought. What if I died? Where would my gay ass go? I stopped reaching out to Jeremy and stopped returning his calls as quickly, and just let things fizzle out.

At the turn of the semester, one of my best friends came back from studying abroad and asked my roommate, "Whatever happened to that guy Brian was dating?" I'll never forget what my straight, frat-boy roommate told me when recounting the conversation: "He was really nice and fun. But you know Brian... He Brian'ed. From what I saw, he got in his head, panicked, and ended it."

My roommate saw what I couldn't see: shame was controlling my life. It didn't just sabotage my dating life, it undermined my relationship with my family. It consumed my thoughts. How many hours and hours did I spend thinking about my sexuality—trying to ignore it, looking for ways to change or control it, researching and rationalizing it?

Recognizing the divine that is already present in your life—including your sex life and your relationships of all sorts—is one key component to thoroughly ridding yourself of shame. Whether you are queer or straight, monogamous or non-monogamous, proactively replacing sex-negative messages with positive stories of sacred sexuality is part of the process of building a thriving life. Cal Newport is a Georgetown University computer science professor and non-fiction author who writes extensively on the toll modern technology takes on our ability to focus, produce deep work, and enjoy meaningful lives. In his book *Digital Minimalism*,[17] he proposes that "social media detoxes" alone are insufficient to break our addictive relationship with apps and devices that research has shown increase our stress, decrease our sleep, destroy our focus, and hinder our relationships.

We know we shouldn't indulge, and yet we still do. Deprivation is not enough. You cannot will yourself to simply resist the allure of your smartphone. Instead, Newport insists, you must add new habits and new interests to your life; you must crowd out mindless scrolling.

Similarly, it is not enough to know that sex is natural, healthy, and good. It is not enough to know that open and polyamorous relationships can be just as healthy, fulfilling, and long-lasting as monogamous ones. It is not enough to know that casual sex and casual partners can be deeply fulfilling, too. You need to believe it deep in your gut. You need to crowd out the messages that say, "There's something wrong with me if I desire an additional partner, or a different type of sex, or another way of relating" and replace them with deeply held beliefs that those desires and those relationships are not just "okay" but good. There's a word for something that is very good and deeply meaningful: holy. What if your relationships— the spouses, the exes you think of fondly, your fuckbuddies, your friends with benefits; your primary partners, comet partners, casual partners; your friends and roommates and maybe even your former co-workers—were all holy? Whether you are monogamous, open, polyamorous, or something else entirely, this book will offer you ways to understand that relationships of all sorts are sacred. If you cannot believe that yet, I, and the people whose stories are shared here, will believe it for you. By the end of this book, however, I expect you will have started to see yourself, your relationships, and the possibilities for your future in bold new ways.

To do that, we need a new definition of the sacred. "The sacred" is not limited to mosques and cathedrals; it's not only found in dusty old relics. The sacred is here and now. The sacred is alive. The sacred is relational. Jason Silva says, "Our relationship with the sacred is our relationship with the timeless. The sacred is the answer to the problem of human existence. And what is the problem of human existence? Our finitude."[18] Psychology professor Sheldon Solomon reminds us that we are "simply breathing pieces of defecating meat, no more significant or enduring than a lizard or a potato."[19] There are tried and tested ways of tapping into the sacred, of tuning into something bigger than ourselves, to know that we are mortal, and also to know that this life matters.

Every year, my chosen family and I take a week-long trip to Fire Island. For decades, the Fire Island Pines and Cherry Grove have been LGBTQ+ enclaves, tucked into a car-free section of a tiny island off the coast of Long Island, New York. The heart-center of my chosen family, Josh, started this annual vacation tradition with his best friend before we met. Soon it grew to include a few other friends, including my partner, with a strict "no boyfriends allowed!" rule, before expanding to include the core of this little family that had started to form over the years, boyfriends now included. On a cool Saturday evening in August 2019, I went out for a run along the boardwalks that criss-cross the island. This year's trip was marked with a looming seriousness—Josh's cancer was back and this time it was terminal—and I needed a break to clear my mind. As I ran across the wooden pathways, I couldn't help but imagine all of the LGBTQ+ people, and particularly gay men, who must have walked these same boardwalks over the years. What stories they would tell, if these planks could talk. In the 1950s and 1960s, queer people came here to escape the strangling homophobia of day-to-day life, even in big cities like New York. In the 1970s and 1980s, as the sexual revolution swept America, Fire Island was a place of hope and joy, a vision of how the world could soon be everywhere. And then with the devastation of AIDS in the 1980s and 1990s, queer men came here to heal, and grieve, and sometimes to die. I was not the first queer man to walk along these boardwalks who was losing a dear friend much too soon.

All paths lead to the marina in the center of the Fire Island Pines and there at the Blue Whale Bar, the island's visitors gather for "tea" every evening just before sunset. From the beach and the pool and the private house parties, they stream down the same paths, young and old, drinkers and sober folks, rich and poor. LGBTQ+ people have been walking down these paths to tea every day, every summer, since 1956. Observant Jews gather in a minyan of at least ten Jewish adults to pray one to three times a day; Muslims stop whatever they are doing, wherever they are, to pray five times a day; there is a Mass at most Catholic churches every single day. And here, on Fire Island, there is tea. We raise glasses of punch like communion or Kiddish; we spin to the beat of the DJ like a whirling dervish or a sacred dance circle. On the Sunday evening of that trip, like every summer Sunday evening for as long as I can remember, the Fire Island Pavilion hosted "Showtunes Sundays." Over 100 LGBTQ+ people were crammed into this island bar singing along to showtunes, led by our mistress of ceremonies, the drag queen Bubbles De Boob.

That year, I walked into the venue just as "You Will Be Found" from the Broadway musical *Dear Evan Hansen* was blaring over the speakers, but you could hardly hear the recording; Ben Platt's voice was drowned out by the chorus of queer voices gathered that evening. The song is about feeling isolated and alone, and then slowly finding meaningful connection, and ultimately the acceptance of a supportive community. It's about hope in the face of fear, and the power of friendship and community to stave off sadness and isolation. I was overwhelmed at how boisterously the crowd was belting out these lyrics in unison. This message, sung by these people, in this place. For generations, LGBTQ+ people have been finding themselves and each other. And we've been doing it together in bookshops and backrooms and bars, just like the Fire Island Pavilion I stood in now. I looked around and thought: this is church. Jason Silva said that "in response to this existential quaking annihilation, this realization that we are mortal beings, the only response is the religious impulse, is a contention with the sacred, which is a contention with the unknown and strive to make it known."[20] The *Evan Hansen* song is a sermon and we were both the church choir and the congregation. There, on that tiny sliver of land in the Long Island Sound, we found ourselves and found each other. (We'll talk more about the power of creating your own spiritual and relational rituals, like the weekly rhythms of Fire Island, in Chapter 9.)

If you, like me, have ever found yourself somewhere not particularly religious—a dinner with your extended polycule full of laughter and love, the dance floor of a club surrounded by friends and lovers, a quiet moment at home with your family—and you've noticed a tingle on the back of your neck, you've taken a deep breath and marveled at just how unbelievably lucky you are, you've settled into a deep and quiet appreciation for what you are in the midst of, I'd like to propose that in those moments, you were having a religious experience. Rabbi Abraham Joshua Heschel[21] wrote, "Wonder or radical amazement is the chief characteristic of the religious [person's] attitude toward history and nature." He goes on to say:

> The meaning of awe is to realize that life takes place under wide horizons, horizons that range beyond the span of an individual life or even the life of a nation, a generation, or an era. Awe enables us to perceive in the world intimations of the divine, to sense in small things the beginning of infinite significance, to sense the ultimate in the common and the simple; to feel in the rush of the passing the stillness of the eternal.

The way polyamorous people relate to one another is a small thing of infinite significance.

Polyamory for me, and for the hundreds of clients I've worked with, is full of awe and wonder. Our private moments with our partners or polycules provide unique insights into the sacred, which we will explore together over the course of this book. Our communal experiences are daily reminders of the "awe and wonder" that almost every polyamorous person has experienced at one point or another. The *Multiamory* podcast is one of the central resources for modern polyamory and in the private Facebook group for the show's supporters, members will regularly ask, "Has anyone else ever…" with dozens of supportive, understanding comments in reply. Every conversation I have with polyamorous clients and community members is brimming with awe and wonder: of our partners and also of the abundant possibilities this style of relating has clued us into. You have been found. The moment you realized non-monogamy was an option for you? That's a revelation. When you gather together with other non-monogamous folks at conferences, in podcast discussion groups, in online communities, and at in-person meetups? Those are sacred communities. You are making meaning out of your life and you are talking about it with others. That is theology—*theo-logos*, god talk. That is holy work. Just as traditional religious movements have sages and sacred texts, so too does non-monogamy, if you'll look at our communities through a faith-filled lens.

What makes a text sacred?

Just about everyone who has been intentionally non-monogamous for some significant period of time has read or at least been recommended *The Ethical Slut* by Dossie Easton and Janet Hardy.[22] *The Ethical Slut* is a sacred text. In fact, the book's official description on the Penguin Random House website notes it is "widely known as the 'Poly Bible.'" Reading *The Ethical Slut* is, for many people, a rite of passage. It is usually one of the first books polyamorous people recommend to others who are starting out on a non-monogamous journey—much like how potential converts to a new religion are advised to read that faith's sacred texts. Much like a religious text, not all polyamorous and non-monogamous people agree with everything written in *The Ethical Slut*. Parts of it are very much a product of their time. We wrestle with what it says. We discard what no longer fits. We adapt what it says for our own personal context. The third edition of *The Ethical Slut* features new and expanded stories. Many of the pages are marked with cutouts and added commentary.

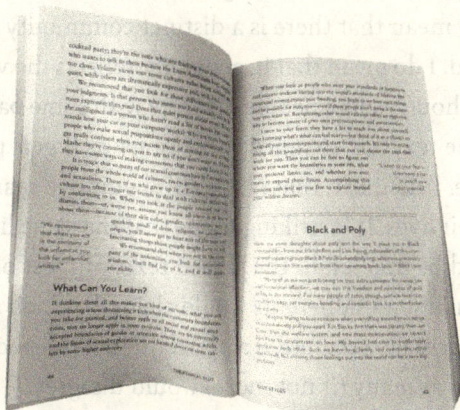

These spreads remind me of a page of the Talmud, where later rabbis discuss the sacred texts of Judaism, sometimes arguing and disagreeing with each other, and providing a wealth of additional perspectives.

If your only association of "the sacred" and "sacred texts" is traditional, institutional religions, you might have some warning bells going off in your head. Here's what I mean—and don't mean—when I say *The Ethical Slut* is a sacred text. I don't mean it's divinely inspired. I don't mean it's a perfect, literal rulebook. I don't mean it's one hundred percent factually accurate. I don't mean its authors are without any personal shortcomings. I don't mean that it is part of a religion. I do mean that there is a distinct community that holds it in high regard. I do mean that it, generally, reflects the values of that group, even though some people disagree with some parts of it. I do mean that the text has changed a few times as it gets passed down through time. I do mean that is a helpful guide to many people in orienting their lives. It is striking to me that the same list of "is" and "is nots" could be applied to the sacred texts of most of the world's religions. While some adherents would claim that their sacred text *is* 100 percent factually accurate, *is* a perfect, literal rulebook, *is* divinely authored, just as many (if not more) would disagree.

If our sacred texts aren't limited to "traditional" texts, whose texts are sacred? That answer is going to vary from person to person, and community to community. Comparative religion author and former Roman Catholic religious sister Karen Armstrong[23] explains in *The Lost Art of Scripture: Rescuing Sacred Texts* that written scripture developed out of oral myth and both are modes to "express a timeless truth that in some sense happened once but which also happens all the time." Sacred scripture helps people to "reach beyond themselves to connect with the true and ultimate reality that will save them from the destructive forces of everyday existence" as American scholar Frederick Streng put it.[24] A sacred text helps us to make meaning out of lives and to live into our deepest values. *The Ethical Slut* meets that criteria for me. I'd like to propose that spending some time thinking about what is sacred to *you* is a worthwhile endeavor. This is an opportunity to have an even greater appreciation for the influences that shaped you. Not sure where to start? Here are some examples of "sacred texts" I've seen for different communities.

Many queer men born in the 1980s and 1990s remember watching *Queer as Folk*. Some of us snuck downstairs to watch it while the rest of the family was asleep. Some had to illegally download it on peer-to-peer file sharing sites like Kazaa and Limewire to watch it. There's a parallel—though with much less serious consequences—to Jews furtively lighting menorahs or Christians owning Bibles in places and times when doing so was illegal. We will go to great lengths to find and connect with the texts that make us feel whole and connect us to our communities. For queer women of a certain age, *The L Word*, *Buffy the Vampire Slayer*, or even not-explicitly-gay shows *Xena: Warrior Princess* are their community's sacred texts. Other sacred texts might include the writings of James Baldwin and Audre Lorde, or the *Queers Read This* pamphlet[25] published anonymously and distributed by members of Queer Nation at New York City Pride in 1990. That pamphlet begins with the iconic line:

How can I tell you. How can I convince you, brother,
sister that your life is in danger: That everyday you wake
up alive, relatively happy, and a functioning human being,
you are committing a rebellious act. You as an alive and
functioning queer are a revolutionary.

While there are some texts that are clearly defined and widely accepted—the Christian Bible, the Koran, the Bhagavad Gita, the Torah, *The Ethical Slut*—there also exists a class of writings that are deeply meaningful to parts of the community but don't quite rise to the same level. In Judaism, the writings of sages such as Maimonides, Spinoza, the Lubavitch rebbes, or Abraham Joshua Heschel come to mind. In Christianity, there are texts accepted as canon by Orthodox and Roman Catholic Churches but not by Protestants (and to a lesser extent, non-canonical writings and gospels that individual Christians and communities find meaningful). In non-monogamous circles, the books *Opening Up, Sex at Dawn, Mating in Captivity*, and *Polysecure* are widely read and recommended. Sacred writing goes beyond codified, printed books, and sacred art extends to other mediums as well. There's poetry, prose, songs, paintings, and other artistic renderings of a community's beliefs and values and how we understand our relationship to each other, our values, and something bigger than ourselves. There is a certain type of painting of Jesus, which many have dubbed "White Jesus": he has straight, flowing light brown or dark blonde hair, he has blue eyes, and most strikingly for someone who was a Middle Eastern Jew, pale white skin. This "White Jesus" painting is historically inaccurate. Some Christians find it mildly annoying, others deeply offensive. There is also a certain type of polyamorous stock photo: three pairs of legs extend from under the sheets beyond the edge of the bed, two sets have painted nails, one has hairy legs (we're supposed to imagine two women and one man), all are white. That stock photo is the "White Jesus" of polyamory sacred art. It's everywhere, it's inaccurate, most of us hate it, but for a long time, it was *the* accepted interpretation.

The prophet is an integral part of many sacred traditions, and non-monogamous communities have those, too. While I'm sure they would shy away from the title, it's hard to ignore the pivotal—prophetic, even—role that many polyamory podcasters and online educators have played in the lives of non-monogamous people: Cunning Minx, host of first-ever polyamory specific podcast *Poly Weekly*; Dedeker Winston, Emily Matlack, and Jase Lindgren, hosts of *Multiamory*; Kevin Patterson of *Poly Role Models*; and Leanne Yau, the polyamory educator and content creator of *Poly Philia*. Even not-polyamorous-specific teachers such as Esther Perel and John and Julie Gottman serve prophet-like roles in our communities.

I'd like to propose that you don't need the Bible, the Koran, or the

Bhagavad Gita, and you don't have to listen to Buddhist monks chant or stand looking up at the ceiling art in the Sistine Chapel to get a glimpse of divine. You can just go on X (formerly known as Twitter).

There are corners of social media sites such as X and Bluesky where queer men create "alts"—alternative, somewhat anonymous accounts—to find each other and post sexually explicit reflections, photos, and videos and to follow adult performers. Psalm 63:1 says, "You, God, are my God, earnestly I seek you; I thirst for you, my whole being longs for you." That psalm sounds to me much like when adult content creator @noahwaybabes said, about having sex with a man with the biggest dick he'd ever seen: "I'm going to spend the rest of my life chasing this high."[26] There are men who talk about receiving cum shots with the same reverence Catholics talk about receiving communion. In communion, you receive bread and wine into your body and though it is only bread and wine, it represents something bigger than that. In Roman Catholic theology, the bread and wine literally transform into the body and blood of Jesus. You are receiving his flesh and fluid into your body and you are transformed in the process. Likewise, adult performer Jonah Wheeler talks in similarly spiritual language about the transformation that can happen through a sexual encounter—whether with a partner or a stranger:

> There's a fantasy version of this that having a part of someone's DNA changes you a little bit. But I also like the idea of spiritually or psychologically you become a little bit like the people through this closeness and this intimate act.[27]

Jonah even used the word "communion" to describe how a sex party, when it is at its best, is joy and compersion* for so many people,

---

*Compersion is happiness caused by another person's joy, especially by seeing one's romantic or sexual partner interacting positively with another one of their partners.

even for strangers. When I asked Jonah to say more about the energy exchange that happens at a sex party, he told me a completely unexpected story: of a time he reached out to a bunch of friends to come together and play bits and pieces of in-progress musical scores. Thirty friends gathered and they had a full orchestra, with him at the center conducting. He likened this to his experience of being in the center of a gangbang. In his ad hoc orchestra party, each player was deeply in tune with the others in their section, paying close attention to the conductor in the center, but also aware of and playing off everyone present, the players in every section. The same was true when he was the central figure in group sex. There were people paying most attention to him, but also interacting with others close by, and everyone feeding off the energy of everyone else in the room. That also sounds like worship to me. Where a room full of people have gathered for a central purpose: to offer a contribution of their energy toward a central figure; where each person is having their own one-on-one experience with that figure but are also intimately aware of and in tune with the people immediately next to them; and where everyone is fed and nourished by the energy of everyone else in the room. Spirit and body mix together. You might even hear moans or sighs. Come, let us worship.

You, too, have probably already tasted a bit of the sexual mixing with the sacred. When we talk about the things that matter most to us, we can't help but rise to poetry. Metaphor is how we make meaning. If you've ever had sex, you've probably heard or said "Oh my God!" many times. We can't help but instinctually know that sex and relationships are inherently sacred. Speaking of God, *what about God*?

CHAPTER 3

A Polyamorous God

As we continue, it feels important to define some terms. If you grew up anywhere with access to American media, your understanding of faith, spirituality, and especially "God," is likely informed by a very particular, relatively modern, movement of media-savvy conservative Christians. If you grew up with a specific, non-Christian religion or live in a part of the world where Christianity is not the dominant religion, you may be lucky enough to have received some alternate ideas that add nuance to what we mean when we talk about the divine. But given the reach of American media and two millennia of aggressive, often violent, Christian proselytizing, it's hard to find an area of the world untouched by conservative beliefs about who and what God is and what we mean when we talk about faith, religion, spirituality, and the sacred. This is true even, sometimes especially, for those of us who didn't grow up particularly religious and may even identify as atheist but who are nonetheless culturally Christian. In the absence of a strong counter-claim, conservative ideas about morality and divinity often define the conversation of spirituality.

When I talk about God, I'm not talking about a God in the sky.

When I talk about the sacred, I'm not talking about a dusty religious artifact dug up from some far-flung cave. When I talk about spirituality, I'm not (only) talking about the Bible or belief. As we explored in the last chapter, the sacred is our relationship with the timeless, that which is bigger than ourselves, and that which gives our life meaning. But what about God, specifically? What do people mean when they talk about "God"? What do I mean? We'll answer those questions, of course, but more interesting to me are the questions: how does polyamory expand our understanding of God (or the Divine, or Source, or whatever word works for you)? In what ways is God present in polyamorous relationships? How do we reflect the image of the divine and how does that image reflect us?

When it comes to the supernatural, I'm a pretty big skeptic and yet, despite being queer, polyamorous, kinky, and slutty, I'm also religious. But what does that even mean?

I've always had an intense interest in science and an intense interest in the Christian faith that was taught to me by my parents and church. Even though my church taught, and in turn I believed, that Christianity was the one true belief system and that "faith in Jesus" was required for "salvation" (which meant, "getting to heaven"), the religious and ethical systems of my friends also seemed to be right, in some meaningful way, especially for them. Before we get too far into this book, I want to expand our imagination of what "faith," "spirituality," "religion," and even "God" and "salvation" might mean. I've met God in the backroom of a gay club, been blessed by a blowjob, and found salvation in a polyamorous relationship.

For most of us, how we understand our relationship to the divine, to our chosen religion (or our choice to abstain from or reject religion), and to the world around us is a bit of hodgepodge. Part what we were taught in childhood, part what we picked up from friends and the society around us, part what we explored and studied and questioned on our own, part what feels comforting and familiar, part what feels helpful and inspiring. My point here is that I'm not particularly interested in what you believe or how you identify. What I want to offer is that you may already be more spiritual than you realize, you might already have a relationship with the sacred, with God even; it just doesn't look like what we see in the movies or on the news. When you begin to look for the divine already present in your life—to notice it, name it, and celebrate it—your whole life begins to transform. This is an invitation to elevate your relationships.

When you think about God, what do you think about? A man up there, out there? Perhaps on some other spiritual plane of conscious existence? Or perhaps your idea of God isn't quite so discrete, isn't quite so human. A supernatural being, or maybe an energy, or perhaps a force that encompasses all genders, or transcends gender entirely?

For some of us, we imagine God is a person that we can talk to and who will talk back to us. Some people experience that response as a distinct voice, words that only they can hear. For others, the response is more subtle: a sense or a sign. For still others, God doesn't communicate with us, but is there nonetheless, gently guiding the events of history. Maybe God set up the universe and put this whole cosmic drama into motion. For some of us, God is fickle and vengeful. God will punish us if we act the wrong way (or think the wrong thing). Or God is a positive energy that vaguely has our back in ways that we're not quite sure of (at least we think so, most of the time). For still others, God is the sum of all that is. When we talk about God, especially when those of us who are skeptics talk about God, it's easy to fall into a post-Enlightenment discussion of the nature or existence of God (for the record: I'm a big fan of the Enlightenment and all the scientific and social progress that is possible because of it). You might ask questions like:

- Does God exist?
- Can we prove (or disprove) that?

But too often we rush to asking "Does God exist?" without first defining who or what we are asking about.

In Hinduism, the world's third-largest religion, there are approximately 330 million gods. Christian theologian Aquinas and Jewish theologian Maimonides both proposed that we can only ever know God by what God is not, rather than being able to affirmatively describe God. In the Torah, there are seven proper names for God, and dozens more titles and metaphors. Kohenet Avra Shapiro compiled a list of 55 names for the divine* which include:

1. Adonai—The One Who Calls the Shots
2. Eloheinu—Our (multi-gendered) God
3. Kadosh Baruch Hu—Holy Blessed One
4. Avinu/Imeinu—Our Parent
5. HaGadol (HaGedolah)—The Big One
6. El Nora (Nora'ah)—The Great One/The One Who Inspires Awe
7. El Elyon—Highest God
8. Eli—My God
9. Yedid Nefesh—Soulmate
10. Melech/Malka—Sovereign One/Queen
11. Tzuri—My Rock.

The Apache gods, *diyí*, are seen as natural forces.[28] The Ojibwe, Cherokee, and Blackfeet nations are also among Native American tribes with diverse gods. Queer Muslim author Amrou Al-Kadhi points out that according to the Quran, the diversity of God is reflected in the diversity of creation. Reflecting on 30:22, "of His signs is the creation of the heavens and earth and the differences of your tongues and colours," Al-Kadhi says "variance and difference among human bodies

---

*For the full list, go to www.kohenetavrashapiro.com/resources

was all part of Allah's plan."[29] Who God is and what role God or the Gods play is understood differently between different communities but also within communities as beliefs change over time, different people have different understandings, and the meaning or role one emphasizes varies from situation to situation. Taken together, while there are vocal celebrity preachers and conservative politicians who claim to know exactly God's will, a close look at the world's religious sages throughout time will reveal that, in general, they are not too concerned with precisely defining God, forever and for always with one exact, scientific explanation of who and what God is. For me, the idea of God is that of a figure, source, entity, idea, or ideal that is central to an individual or community and to whom the individual or community can turn to for strength, support, insight, and guidance. That could be a very specific, personal, almost anthropomorphic God, or God could be, like some of my friends in Alcoholics Anonymous say, a "Group of Drunks." In all cases, God is that-which-is-bigger-than-ourselves, though what *exactly* that *is* will vary from person to person and community to community.

Humans have a tendency, when attempting to describe that which is beyond the reach of our ordinary language, to naturally shift to impassioned, poetic language. ("The rise to poetry" is what we call this when it happens in theatre.) That's what happened with the writers of sacred scripture and that's what still happens, thousands of years later, centuries of scientific advancement be damned, when we try to describe *that-which-is-greater-than-ourselves.*

What happens when we see a sunset, when we hold a newborn, when we join with others in song, when we march for justice, when we have sex with a beloved partner.

Just one month after my partner and I decided to open up our relationship, we were at a New York City gay bar, a few days before the end of the year. It was that liminal time of year between Christmas and New Year's Day when the days blur together and many people take time off work. As the night drew on and the lights dimmed and the drinks flowed, I couldn't help but notice Dominic, a cute friend of friends I hadn't met yet, tucked in on the dance floor. Every few seconds, the dance floor lighting would streak across his face and his eyes would glisten. At least, that's how I remember it. Slowly, we began to writhe and shimmy our way across the dance floor. First dancing next to each other and then, decidedly, *with* each other. His hand wrapped around my waist and he pulled me closer. I reached for his shoulder and ran my fingers through the back of his hair. I could feel the hum of energy buzzing through my body. I could feel sparks leap from his hip to mine, as we rocked together in motion to the beat. But there weren't any sparks, there wasn't any electricity, was there? We were vibing but the only literal vibrations were those of the sound waves through the air. There are the facts of what is happening: light rays hitting the back of our eyes, matter touching the nerves on our skin, sound waves vibrating in our ear canal, hearts pumping faster, bodies sweating, pupils dilating. But there is also something else happening: beauty, awe, chills, passion, connection, intimacy, transcendence. We are a collection of atoms and we are so much more.

Dancing with Dominic was like riding a roller coaster. Our eyes met and time slowed down, the background behind him dimmed and blurred, the roar of the crowd faded down. I wanted to kiss him. I realized, however, that my partner and I had not talked about how to handle kissing or hooking up with mutual friends and I wasn't sure who here knew that we were open. I didn't want to start making out with this guy in front of all of Peter's friends if they might get the wrong impression or if it would make Peter uncomfortable. So we didn't kiss. We'd lock eyes and lean in and let our lips linger ever so close but not quite touching. *Spark. Sizzle.* Then we'd break our trance and the lights and sound and din of the club would come roaring back. And then, eventually, our eyes would lock again and the cycle would repeat. It was transcendental. To this day, saying "that was transcendental" whenever there is a particularly special moment has become a bit of an inside joke between me and my partner, calling back to my recollection of that night on the dance floor.

Whenever I'm at a dance club with my queer friends, I like to take a break to grab some water and fresh air. When I return to the dance floor, before jumping back into the action, I linger a little on the edge. I gaze out on to the floor and spot my friends. They're dancing not just with their partners, but also with their friends. I watch them shower each other with physical affection: hugs and kisses, winks and nods, silly faces and singing along, pinched cheeks, and even making out. Casually they throw their arms around each other in hugs and embraces while they ebb and flow, dancing in a circle, grinding against each other, weaving in and out, finding new friends to hug and sing along with, and even to kiss. If you squint your eyes just right, you can see the Holy Spirit right there on the dance floor of a queer club. In these moments, my intense focus on my friends and the strangers who fill the dance floor, my intentional remembering of all the people who have danced to music just like this for ages and ages, my appreciation for how precious it is that we can live and dance and flirt queerly and non-monogamously in public safely, it is awe-some. I am full of awe. I had this intuitive sense that I could see God on the dance floor of queer clubs for years before I read the works of Abraham Joshua Heschel. For Heschel, our perception of awe and wonder are deeply intertwined—synonymous, even—with our experience of the divine. In *I Asked for Wonder: A Spiritual Anthology*, he wrote:[30]

> Awe is an intuition for the dignity of all things, a realization that things not only are what they are but also stand, however remotely, for something supreme. Awe is a sense for transcendence, for the reference everywhere to mystery beyond all things. It enables us

to perceive in the world intimations of the divine. ...to sense the ultimate in the common and the simple: to feel in the rush of the passing the stillness of the eternal. What we cannot comprehend by analysis, we become aware of in awe.

I don't know how to define the nature of God. I can't put God in a bottle or under a microscope. I can't measure God with a machine (would it be like the ones Scientologists use? Surely not!). There's nothing in what we know about the universe—and we know a lot, even though there is also a lot we don't understand—to suggest that there is a conscious outside entity that interferes in our affairs to bend or break the laws of nature, to guide the course of human affairs. God did not give you that touchdown or clear skies on your wedding day or save your aunt from cancer and if God did, what would it say about all the people who didn't make the touchdown, who had rain on their wedding day, who died from cancer? But I meet God on the dance floor every time I go to a queer club. Many of my friends say that God helped to rescue them from the clutches of devastating addiction. I, by myself, am not God. I have stood on protest lines, held vigils and gone toe-to-toe with virulently anti-LGBTQ+ religious leaders to proclaim the good news of the queer gospel and I have *felt something in my bones*. Jesus says in Matthew 18 that where two or three are gathered, there he is too. When people believe in something together and come together for a common cause, something happens that is greater than the sum of its parts. Something divine happens in community.

I don't believe that there is a conscious force outside the universe bending it to its will, and yet I believe that "the arc of the moral universe is long, but it bends towards justice" (as Rev. Dr. Martin Luther King, Jr. said, paraphrasing Theodore Parker). Not because an outside force bends it, not because it must bend, but because *we bend it*. I believe that love wins and justice prevails not because a puppet-master on high decrees that it must, but because something in our very nature is primed for love and justice, because something that you can feel even if you can't quite measure happens when humans come together, when we help each other, when we do what is right, when we are willing to sacrifice for a higher cause.

Whatever *that* is... That connection, that longing, that energy, that urge; that which draws us outside ourselves; that which courses through us with the same energy that has been coursing through all the universe since the Big Bang; that thing which is—much like light, which is somehow *both* a particle and a wave—two things at once, exactingly, precisely physical right down to the atoms that make us up (from stardust we are and to stardust we shall return) and also completely unmeasurable but no less real (spiritual, we might say). *That* is what humans throughout the ages have called God. And I believe *that God* is within us and among us and for us.

I believe that polyamory and other forms of non-monogamy help us to understand God more fully. There is a line from the Talmud that is often referenced in Jewish study: "Ben Bag-Bag used to say of the Torah: Turn it and turn it again, for everything is in it. Pore over it, and wax gray and old over it" (Pirkei Avot 5:25).[31] We must keep turning to look for God. For the first eight years of QueerTheology.com, my co-host and creative partner Fr. Shannon T.L. Kearns I followed the Christian lectionary and offered a queer perspective on one of the lectionary passages each week. The Christian lectionary has a repeating three-year cycle (with some passages repeating yearly), which means we went through the whole thing nearly three times. During our 12 years on the air, we have covered many passages multiple times. We often say that our sacred texts are one way that we can understand God and that these texts—and God, Godself—are a bit like an onion: there is always another layer to peel back, a new insight to have. Each time we come to the text, we see something new. More than that, Shannon and I often see something different in the text and in the divine. His experiences as a transgender man show me something of the divine I would never know on my own, as do my experiences as a polyamorous person, as do James Cones's insights as a Black theologian and Pamela Lightsey's as a womanist theologian, to name just two thinkers who have inspired and informed me.

It is not that polyamorous people have the highest insight into the divine, it's that we have our own unique insight and we need to add that particular insight into the chorus of other voices, indigenous voices, disabled voices, voices from the Global South, HIV-positive voices, immigrant voices, transgender voices, womanist and feminist voices, incarcerated voices, terminally ill voices—the list goes on. I could not possibly list all the perspectives on the divine; that is why we must keep turning it and turning it again. You have a unique insight into the divine that only you have. We need you to add your voice. We need the full chorus of voices to fully understand God.

God cannot be contained in boxes or neat and tidy labels, and God can also not be contained in just one chapter. In the next section of this book, we'll look at some pillars of both religious life and relational life and see how a polyamorous perspective sheds new light on these. As we turn and turn these well-worn topics, the divine will show up in new and unexpected ways. Let's go looking.

A polyamorous wedding at Mount Sinai

I can't help but think that God is a little bit polyamorous.

While monotheism is a central part of Jewish faith, when I look at God's relationship with the Jewish people, I see some polyamory there. Shavuot is one of the three major pilgrimage festivals in Judaism. Described and commanded in the Torah, it originally was a time where Jews would travel to the temple in Jerusalem to make offerings at the beginning of the wheat harvest. Over time, the holiday also began to take on a commemoration of the revelation of the Torah to the Jewish people at Mount Sinai. For centuries, if not longer, many Jews have seen Shavuot as a sort of marriage between Adonai and the Jewish people. For one, the Tanakh is filled with romantic metaphors. *Song of Songs*, which is, on its face, an epic and sexually explicit poem about two unmarried lovers, is understood by many to be a metaphor for the relationship between God and the Jewish people, or God and all of humanity. In Hosea 2, speaking of the Jewish people, God is recounted as saying, "And I will betroth* you forever." The language of marriage is right there. At the start of Shavuot services, many Sephardic communities read from a *ketubah*—a marriage contract—between God and Israel. There are highly decorative *ketubot* between God and the people of Israel that mirror the ones Jewish couples have made for their weddings for millennia. In the climax of the story of revelation at Mount Sinai, Exodus 24 describes the scene: "Then [Moses] took the Book of the Covenant and read it to the people. They responded, 'We will do and hear everything the Lord has said.'" We will do. I do. A wedding vow between Adonai and the people of Israel. In all these metaphors, the People of Israel are seen as one collective, to whom God is wedded. I take my place as just one part of a greater whole seriously. And also, if there is a marriage and we are all part of it, then that's polyamory!

Jesus is polyamorous

Christianity, too, has a polyamorous God. Jesus is polyamorous. For Christians who believe in a "personal relationship with Jesus," I have some news for you: like Adonai at Sinai, Jesus is in a personal relationship with billions of other people, too. That's not what I mean

*Also translated as "espouse."

when I say Jesus is polyamorous, though, because of course there are lots of different types of multi-person relationships that don't fall under the polyamory umbrella: friends, family, co-workers. When I say that Jesus is polyamorous, I don't mean that Jesus *was* polyamorous; instead, I'm making a present-tense theological claim: Jesus *is* polyamorous. While you won't find the Bible detailing Jesus's literal polyamorous exploits, if you approach the Bible with a polyamorous lens, you'll find that polyamory has been in the text all along. In Ephesians 5, the author specifically uses the word "marriage" to describe Christ's relationship with the fledgling Christian community (and presumably, with all of Jesus's followers since). Paul writes, "Marriage is a significant allegory, and I'm applying it to Christ and the church." Repeatedly, Paul reminds his readers that Jesus gave himself for the world and even more specifically, for the "Church," which he describes as "the whole body of believers."* In this marriage, Jesus isn't married to one person, he is married to the entire body of believers. Jesus is in a pansexual, polyamorous relationship!

The importance of a polyamorous God

I hope that we already recognize that God's love for us isn't diminished by God's love for other people. In every religious tradition, and outside formal religious traditions, each of us can have a unique, transcendent relationship with the divine. God's relationship with you is not diminished by others' relationship with God. It feels worth exploring the ways in which God could be polyamorous because, for millennia, monogamous, heterosexual, patriarchal marriage has served as a ubiquitous metaphor for God's relationship to us. That influences both what we think about God and also what we think

---

*In Ephesians 5:30, Paul says of the church that "we are parts of [Christ's] body."

about our relationships. We make and celebrate these connections because, as Judith Plaskow[32] said in her seminal Jewish feminist work *Standing Again at Sinai*:

> To speak of God is to speak of what we value most. In attributing certain qualities to God, we both attempt to point to God and offer God's qualities to be emulated and admired. To say that God is just, for example, is to say both that God acts justly and that God demands justice.

If God is and must be monogamous, does that mean God loves some people more than others? Does it mean that God acts jealously, even possessively, even violently? Certainly, there are people who believe all those things about God. Do you? If God is or could be polyamorous, how might you understand God's qualities differently? Could God have more than enough love for every single person? Could God be a God with whom you negotiate and co-create the boundaries, structures, and agreements of your relationship and have a regular relationship check-in as many relationships do? (More on that in Chapters 7 and 9.) Could your relationship with God be structured differently from someone else's relationship and yet both still be meaningful? What kind of God do *you* believe in?

A polyamorous perspective on God also changes my relationship to the people around me. My neighbors are not just my neighbors, they are also my metamours (partner's partners). Miriam isn't just a prophet I can admire, she's my sisterwife! In some meaningful way, we are already family. Polyamorous people don't always get along with their partner's partners, in just the same way you might not always get along with everyone at church, synagogue or mosque. Parallel polyamory is a style of relating where one's other partners exist in close proximity to one another (by obvious necessity) but they aren't integrated or even intersected. They run next to each other, like parallel railroad tracks. While in parallel polyamory, you don't have to love or even get along with your partner's other partners, they do still exist and you have the ability to affect each other through your shared relationship with your mutual partner. I don't have much in common with some sects of Orthodox Jews, but HaShem is our hinge partner: we're both in a deep, committed, loving, and long-term relationship with the same entity. So we'd better figure out how to get along well enough!

Our imagination of God as polyamorous can also help enrich our approach to non-monogamous relationships. You know how you feel good when something good happens to someone you care about? If you are someone who has found deep meaning in your relationship with the divine or with faith and spirituality, have you ever felt the impulse of wanting to share that good news with others in your life? That is how I feel about my partners. They are pretty awesome! Why would I not want others to be blessed by them too? There are times when something exciting happens to a friend, neighbor, or co-worker: a new job, a new relationship, discovering a new passion, or something else that makes them light up. In these moments, it can seem as if God is blessing them. I, personally, don't subscribe to a theology of a fickle God doling out good things to some people some of the time, but I can nonetheless appreciate the imagery of "blessings" in our lives. When others are blessed, it blesses me to share in their joy. We can join in celebrating the good things that happen to the people we care about precisely because we care about them. Their joy does not take away from ours. This is how I feel when my partners connect with someone new. There is more joy, love, and excitement in their lives. I can join in celebrating this precisely because I care about them.

CHAPTER 4

Love

On a warm summer day in New York City, I was walking down the subway stairs at Fifth Avenue in Manhattan having spent an afternoon in Central Park with a guy I was newly dating. He cracked some dorky joke and pulled an absolutely adorable face and I exclaimed, without even thinking, "Oh my God, I love you!" It's a phrase I've said countless times before to friends or family when they do something delightful, but in the context of a romantic relationship, the word "love" hung in the air like the humidity in the below-ground subway station.

"I mean...not like, 'I love you, *like that*' you know. You know what I mean?!" I quickly clarified.

We had never said "I love you" to each other before. But then I paused as the flurry of thoughts and emotions I'd been sitting with over the past weeks raced in my head. "*Not like that*" didn't quite feel right either. I swallowed. "You know, I take that back. I *do* love you. There are lots of different types of love and maybe it's too soon to say 'I'm *in love* with you' but in some of the ways that we can love, I *do* already love you." He smiled that adorable smile and replied, "I know what you mean. Maybe too soon for being *in love* for forever, but I love you too." And then he grabbed my hand and hurried me into the nearby subway car.

You can love your partner of 20+ years and you can love the person you have been dating for a few months and you don't have to love them exactly the same for them both to be love. One time, at 2am, I was in the middle of having sex with a man I'd met on the hookup app Sniffies just 20 minutes prior and I almost said "I love you" to him. Though I didn't even know his name, we were sharing an intensely deep connection and as we locked into each other's eyes and the sweat dripped from my face on to his chest, I could feel the words "I love you" welling up in my chest. Something profound was happening. Time was standing still; we had become immortal gods to each other, as Roland Barth would say about love and lust.[33] My impulse to say "I love you" was an impulse to name the ecstatic experience I was having. While I was editing this book, I met up with a different man, in a different city, from the same Sniffies app and on our second meetup, as we were approaching climax, he did say, through panting breath, "I love you, Brian!" Afterwards, I told him about this book and the story of how I almost said it once before. He shared that when he's having sex with someone, he feels an intense connection with the person. He used to ignore those feelings but now rather than shove them down, he gives voice to them. When the sex is over, he doesn't actually expect any love or commitment from the partner, but in the moment, it is a recognition of the intensity of the connection being shared and the meaningfulness of it, even if it only lasts half an hour. Anonymous, non-monogamous sex can be sacred, too.

In Greek, which much of the Christian New Testament was written in, there are at least three major words for love: *philios* (sibling love), *eros* (erotic love), and *agape* (a self-sacrificing type of love). The "I love you" I almost said to the anonymous hookup is different from the "I love you" I said on the subway platform, different from the "I love you" I said to my husband during our wedding vows, different from the "I love you" I say to my friends as we say goodbye after dinner. I like the idea that love is too big to be captured by just one word. This too-big-for-one-word idea of love is embedded into many religious traditions. In the Koran,[34] there are two different words for two different types of God's love: *rahma* and *hub*. In Hebrew, *ahavah* is the most common word for love but there are others. There's *chesed* which is a benevolent kind of love, often translated as lovingkindness. It's the love-power with which God created the world.[35] You see it in modern Hebrew and throughout the Hebrew Bible, including Psalm 89:2, "Your steadfast love is confirmed forever," which inspired the activist song "Olam Chesed Yibaneh," a call to build a better world from a place of love. There's also *dod*, which appears most famously in *Song of Songs* and is often in wedding vows, including my own:

אֲנִי לְדוֹדִי וְדוֹדִי לִי
Ani l'dodi, v'dodi li
"I am my beloved's and my beloved is mine."

Even in my work with people who are spiritual-but-not-religious or completely secular, "love" is often expressed as one of the highest virtues. You might even sometimes see Love capitalized, to represent its place as The Most Important Value.

Given the limitations of English, it's often not enough to just say "love." We have developed a variety of words, phrases, and metaphors to help us capture the precise flavor of love. In English-speaking, monogamy-centric culture, we rely on context to define which type of love we mean when we say "I love you." Is it to a spouse? A co-worker? A friend? A family member? Like Biblical Hebrew and Greek, polyamorous people and communities also know some things about the too-big-for-one-word-ness of love (and also the too-big-for-one-person-ness of it). We have come up with different terminology to describe and differentiate the feelings that arise with a new partner versus the feelings you have for a long-term established partner: New Relationship Energy (NRE) and Old or Established Relationship Energy (ERE). The skipping of my heart and the anxiety of "how is he going to respond?" as I stumbled over "I love you" on that subway platform: that was NRE. When my husband knows what I'm asking before I finish the question or when we lie in bed next to each other, reading different books, but with one hand resting gently on each other's thigh: that is ERE. There's "compersion" for the feel-good feelings you get in response to your partner's love and joy for their other partner(s). And of course we coined the term "polyamory" itself: a kind of expansive, abundant love that is big enough for multiple partners. In coining new words for different types of love, polyamorous communities join with other religious traditions to add new words to the sacred lexicon.

One year in my middle school youth group, we had a three-part series on love, sex, and relationships. One whole lesson was devoted to "Apple Pie Love" versus "Twue Love" (the latter, a reference to a line from the movie *The Princess Bride*). The idea behind "Apple Pie Love versus Twue Love" is that there are some things you might say you love, for instance, apple pie, but they are sweet and tempting and not particularly nutritious and if you eat too much, you'll get a tummy ache. While there is another kind of love—Twue Love—that is found in the context of (monogamous, heterosexual) marriage that is deeply fulfilling and long-lasting in satisfaction. The lesson was: pursue Twue Love and don't get distracted by Apple Pie Love. Even conservative Christians recognize there are multiple ways to love; they just choose to value some over others. It strikes me that Twue Love and Apple Pie Love are just other ways of describing ERE and NRE. It's not true though that Twue Love and Apple Pie Love are in opposition to one another. They're both meaningful and sometimes, even, one can turn into the other. When you're in the early days of a new relationship, you want to feast on the other person—metaphorically and sometimes literally. In the same way you can only eat so much delicious apple pie (or, in my case a box of Entenmann's crumb topped donuts), before you get sick, you can also only stay up until 3am having sex, talking about your deepest secrets, and making wild dreams for the future for so many days or weeks before eventually you need sleep and to return to a normal schedule. Whether you call it New Relationship Energy or Apple Pie Love, it's not going to last forever, but that doesn't mean it's cheap, meaningless, or unimportant.

As you see throughout this book, casual flings and fleeting dates, not just long-term relationships, can be deeply meaningful, even sacred. Even in Twue Love, ERE relationships, many clients I work with want to recapture the ecstatic, uncontrollable sexual energy of the early days of their relationship. The Apple Pie Love of their early days was delicious! Even though both NRE and a box of donuts will cause your brain to release lots of dopamine and other feel-good chemicals, that doesn't mean other types of food and other types of love are somehow less important, real, or valuable. They're just different. You can have a passionate love and energetic sex life decades into your relationship, but it probably will, and even should, look and feel different from the "Apple Pie Love" of NRE. It will be less anxious and more grounded. With time, you can go deeper. It's okay if the dessert tastes a little different.

While *eros* is a type of love obviously associated with romantic relationships, it's not the only type of love you experience in your partnerships. The early days, weeks, and even months of a new relationship are usually full of eros. You can't stop thinking about your partner; you want to kiss and embrace and fuck. Psychologists identify this period as "limerence," which *Psychology Today*[36] defines as "a state of involuntary obsession with another person." Many polyamorous people call this feeling New Relationship Energy, while in pop culture it's known simply as "the honeymoon period." Lust and/ or erotic love might be part of limerence, but it's actually something distinct. A key part of limerence is the uncertainty of the relationship and of your desire. Do they desire you back? It turns out that this uncertainty is a powerful driver of erotic desire. Then, over time, limerence, or NRE, fades as your brain and body begin to realize that this relationship is here to stay. Confident that your new mate isn't going anywhere, your brain stops flooding you with chemicals to obsessively chase after this partner so that you can focus on other important areas of your life. If you were staying up until 3am having marathon sex and deep conversations about your innermost feelings *every night*, you would be exhausted and probably eventually get fired from your job for poor performance.

The ending of the honeymoon period can be bittersweet, but it makes way for something deeper: Old Relationship Energy or Existing Relationship Energy. I'd like to propose that this shift from New Relationship Energy to Existing Relationship Energy is also when, in healthy relationships, *agape* love begins to develop, and that polyamorous relationships are particularly suited to teach us all about believing in and living into agape love.

It's not a new idea to think that *agape* might be present in a romantic relationship; even the conservative Christian advocacy group Focus on the Family talks about that. The Focus on the Family website* says, quoting Coty Pinckney:

> Agape is a love that gives, a love that does not demand or hold onto rights, but has the good of the other at heart. This is the love we need to work on in our marriage in order for our spouse to feel like he or she is married to Jesus.

*www.focusonthefamily.com

That's a nice idea, isn't it? (It sounds a lot like polyamory to me.)

If you scratch even a little, you can see that the "rules" of monogamy hem in *agape*. Mandatory monogamy is expressly about "holding on to your rights" over your partner. Mandatory monogamy says that there should be a different type of love for different types of people. This is not untrue; I love my dad and my sister and my boyfriend and my best friend and my ex and my neighbor in different ways. But it is also not completely true either. Sometimes, at best, those distinctions are arbitrary, and sometimes, at worst, they're divisive and harmful. The mere existence of polyamorous relationships testifies to the reality that love can be bigger than one person. There is a section of the Supreme Court ruling which legalized same-gender (monogamous) marriage nationwide which is often read in progressive weddings:

> No union is more profound than marriage, for it embodies the highest ideals of love, fidelity, devotion, sacrifice, and family. In forming a marital union, two people become something greater than once they were.

I bristle every time I hear it. The love, fidelity, devotion, sacrifice, and family that I share with my best friend Matt is equally as profound as my marriage to my husband. The ways I love and cherish my dear friends Asher, Amy, Stacey, Sam, and Shannon through decades and distance is a profound expression of family. Many queer and polyamorous people demonstrate through our lives and loves that romantic love is not, in fact, the highest expression.

This polyamorous and relationship anarchist idea of blurring the boundaries between friends, family, lovers, and spouses can enrich our faith and our whole lives—regardless of how we structure our own personal relationships (we'll explore this more in Chapters 8 and 11). The traditional understanding of marriage and monogamy is that a certain type of love is reserved only for our one spouse. If God's *agape* love is expansive, then monogamous marriage is a limiting metaphor for and example of it. Divine love *must* be bigger than a love limited to only one person, otherwise the Divine is selfish and discriminatory. If we think that our love of our spouse is an analogy for God's love for us and we're supposed to love our spouse more than others, it's a natural extension that God loves some of us more than others.

This plays out in real life: when I was visiting my childhood church as an adult, the preacher actually said, "God loves some of us more than others." I was so shocked and horrified I wrote it down to remind myself later that I hadn't misremembered what he said. It is only human to love some people more than others. As much as I work to "do love" into the world, to be kind, generous, and welcoming to everyone I meet, to be quick to show up for the people in my life, I can't help but subtly and subconsciously love some people more than others. It is hard to not prioritize the comfort of my husband over a stranger I met just moments ago. It's maybe even a *good* thing to have *some* prioritization in your life. If you try to take care of each of the earth's nine billion people, you won't be able to take care of anyone well. Love may be infinite, but time, energy, and resources are not. Sometimes narrowing your focus can help you love more deeply and fully. I would like to propose that this narrowing of focus be an intentional choice rather than our unconscious habit. And I'd like to believe that God is big enough to love us all.

Falling in and out and back in love with God (and/or your spiritual community)

What does it mean to love God or to be loved by God? Loving God is central to Judaism. The commandment from the Torah, in Deuteronomy, to love God with all your heart, soul, strength, and might, is embedded at the very beginning of the Shema, the central prayer of the Jewish people. Many Christian worship songs proclaim their love for God as well as God's love for us. While we will talk later in this chapter about the specifics of putting love into action, and in later chapters of defining what commitment to God could look like, for a moment I want to focus on the *feeling* of love with God. Getting swept up in the feeling of love for God and of being loved by God can be powerful. Many religious services use lights, scents, music, and movement to induce an ecstatic feeling of connection to the divine. Catholicism, Hinduism, Judaism, and Islam all use incense and candles as part of various religious observances. I can't help but notice that the "smells and bells" of a high church service or the fragrant incense and flickering candle lights in a Buddhist temple aren't so different from the colored lights and fog machines in a megachurch. You can see similarities between the holy hands of Protestant worship, shuckling while davening, and dancing at a powwow.* We humans crave not just an intellectual connection with the divine, but also an emotional one—which leaves us feeling particularly vulnerable when it seems as if God has withdrawn from us. In Psalm 22, the author writes:

> My God, my God, why have you forsaken me?
> Why are you so far from saving me, from the words of my groaning?
> O my God, I cry by day, but you do not answer,
> and by night, but I find no rest.

Even the acclaimed Catholic saint, Mother Teresa, wrote in her personal diary,[37] "the place of God in my soul is blank, there is no God

---

*Shuckling is a swaying motion some Jews perform during prayer as a way to enhance concentration. Daven is the Yiddish word for prayer and is used to mean reciting the Jewish liturgical prayers.

in me" and, "I just long and long for God and then it is that I feel he does not want me—he is not there."

As co-founder and director of spiritual practices at QueerTheology.com, I work regularly with people who feel distant and disconnected from God. Many people have had experiences of intense closeness with the divine and are longing to recapture those feelings, while others have *never* felt that way and worry that means something is wrong with them or it is evidence that God does not exist. This is where the polyamorous framework of NRE and ERE can help us make sense of the *feeling* of love for God and being loved by God. There may have been times in your life when you had a particularly meaningful religious experience and felt particularly close to God. This may have been a one-time ecstatic experience like attending a high-energy religious festival or having a particularly meaningful trip on drugs. You might have even experienced it like a conversion of sorts. Conversion experiences have lots of similarities with really incredible first dates. You're in a setting that is outside where you normally spend your time; maybe you've dressed up specially for this particular event. You meet someone new—or you see them again with fresh eyes—and there's a deep and instant attraction. Somehow, over the span of just a few hours, you can suddenly picture your whole life together. Something has shifted. Everything is different.

Not everyone has these peak religious experiences or over-the-moon first dates. For some people, it's a slower burn that then bubbles over in a moment of ultimate knowing. The conversion process to Judaism takes many months or often multiple years. I joke that my conversion journey lasted "two years or two decades, depending on how you count." As I progressed further along, from the first introduction to it through friends' b'nei mitzvah as a tween, to keeping kosher for Passover with a friend at 18, to Hebrew lessons at Hillel with my college roommate, and conversations with close friends about life, values, and ultimate meaning, I continued to feel drawn closer and closer to this particular understanding of and way of interacting with the divine. Eventually, I officially joined the Jewish people through formal conversion, culminating in a *bit dein* and *mikveh*, the rabbinic court and ritual immersion required as the final steps for conversion.

That journey in some way parallels the beginning of my relationship with my now-husband: we started off as friends, began spending more and more time together, started talking about "making it official," and eventually had a moment (or a few moments) of solidifying that commitment. This was first through a verbal commitment to each other and then, 15 years later, through a public ritual commitment and formal, legal marriage.

I see this over and over again: in a healthy relationship, the highs of a new relationship eventually give way to a steady confidence. In fact, a slightly reduced sex drive can actually be a sign of a healthy relationship. In an unstable relationship, one where you are constantly anxious about losing your partner, your brain will *constantly* crave sex with your partner as a way of seeking reassurance that your partner is available and committed. One of the reasons you can't take your hands off your partner whenever you see them in the early days of a relationship is because you are worried that this may be the last time you see them. Sex, our brains have been conditioned to think, will keep them coming back for more. Over time, as you begin to deepen your commitment through explicit commitments, a shared vision for the future, and comforting rituals (all things we will explore in future chapters), your brain chemistry can ease up—a stable relationship replaces insatiable cravings for peak experiences. It's still love, though.

During my formal conversion process and in my first year of being Jewish, everything was new and everything was exciting. I was attending shul weekly, volunteering monthly with our tzedek council to make lunches for the Hollywood Food Coalition, attending seminars and classes, reading dozens of books, and listening to

Jewish-themed podcasts nearly every day. I was like a new lover who just couldn't get enough of it. Shavout is an annual spring holiday traditionally marked by all-night study. I found out that Ikar, a social-justice oriented independent congregation in my neighborhood, was hosting a late-into-the-city program of learning, networking, and discussion. So what did I do? I stayed up until 4am! In discussions with other converts to Judaism, we observed that many of us feel moved to take on the practices of Judaism, such as daily davening, lighting Shabbat candles weekly, some version of keeping kosher, and marking even the less popular Jewish holidays, even if we are part of liberal communities where such obligations are not expected of us. Our working theory was that we do this because they are very specific ways that we can cultivate feeling Jewish and displaying being Jewish. While my friends and family who were born Jewish feel Jewish simply because they have always been Jewish, doing something Jewish can help those of us with an insecure attachment to our Judaism to feel more connected (to borrow a relationship framework).

As the NRE of my relationship with Judaism gives way to a healthy and secure ERE, I still do many of the same things as before, so that I might continue cultivating a relationship with the divine and with my community. That's the same way that people in long-term relationships need to continue dating each other and taking proactive action to support their relationship. But with ERE, it's a stable, confident action, not a clawing, insecure, uncertain one. Here are some ways NRE and ERE might look and feel in your relationship with the divine:

New Relationship Energy	Established Relationship Energy
A kid-in-a-candy-store overwhelmed feeling	Comfortable and cozy, like a favorite blanket or sweatshirt
Disorienting	Familiar

Fleeting	Dependable
An energetic peak, followed by a depressing crash	A rolling ebb and flow of interest and attention
One-off, irregular events. Not sure when you'll encounter it again	Planned, regular rituals for engaging and re-engaging
Impulsive	Considered
Can leave you tired, anxious, or with a "vulnerability hangover" (but still you want more!)	Leaves you feeling rejuvenated and refreshed
A desire to recreate the experience	The safety to explore other ways and places of connecting

In future chapters, I'll share specific strategies for making commitments with your higher power and how to build rituals to support your relationships (both human and divine), but right now I want to help you spot some differences between the NRE and ERE of your relationship. This way, you don't have to worry that you've fallen out of love with God—or that God has fallen out of love with you—and can instead rest easy knowing that you are deeply held by the universe.

Love may be abundant, but time is not. As I have been writing this book, I have planned my wedding with Peter, moved across the country, been a volunteer leader at my synagogue, and taken two family vacations (one with my queer chosen family and one with my family of origin), all while working full time to pay the bills. I have managed to have a hookup every now and then and to keep up with my closest friends and partners but I know that I am at capacity. I am "poly saturated," which means I am at capacity in my ability to make or maintain additional romantic or sexual connections. Love is an ongoing action and you've got to make the time to put in the work that love, in all its diverse forms, requires. While it is easy to imagine how non-monogamous people could become overextended in their relationships, if you're not careful, your time and attention can get pulled away from those you care most about, no matter your relationship structure. In my work as a relationship coach, it is often not outside partners who most threaten a relationship but a chronic neglect from inside the relationship. This neglect is often subtle, it can even be coded as "normal" in relationships, but over time, the effects add up. A subtle neglect can look like spending much of your time at home together, but you are distracted by social media, movies and TV shows, video games, or nightly casual pot smoking or wine drinking. You can crowd out your time with commitments outside the house too: working long hours, living at the gym or the bar, or filling up your social calendar to the detriment of quality time with your partner(s) are common ones I see in my practice. When you add non-monogamy into the mix then time spent on dating and hookup apps, talking with potential partners, and going out on dates and hookups, all take up additional time. If you are not careful, you will end up taking the people you care about most for granted. That is a recipe for disaster.

While grand gestures of love make for dramatic scenes in movies and television shows, big extravagant moves are not what builds deep, lasting love in real life. In my relationship coaching practice, when I work with couples who find their love for one another is strained, they have often tried such big gestures before: a trip to Paris or Vegas, nightly four-hour long conversations to talk about their feelings, moving in together, buying a house together, getting married, even considering having kids together. I understand the impulse: if you have a problem that feels big, you imagine the solution must need to be equally big in scale to solve it. Through my work, I see time and again that it is small, simple actions, repeated over time that contribute to a sense of love, commitment, and security in a romance. Some "actions of love" I often recommend to my client are:

- going for a walk around the block each night, holding hands
- cooking dinner together once a week
- planning a low-cost date night once a month
- turning your phones completely off and leaving them in another room, sitting on the couch facing each other (ideally touching one another), and talking about the most exciting and most challenging parts of your day
- pulling a card from a "questions card deck" during dinner each night and discussing it (I recommend the Intimacy Deck by BestSelf Co.).

The gift of non-monogamy is that these relationship skills transcend relationship structure and are equally effective in monogamous relationships. So then, why are we talking about them here? Non-monogamy can be a stress test of a relationship, exposing areas that need attention. In a monogamous relationship, it can be easy to lean on the social and legal support structures to tough out the relationship. Psychotherapist and relationship expert Jessica Fern observes,[38] "embracing a non-monogamous paradigm can be a powerful catalyst for change that requires partners to both learn new things and address old, dysfunctional patterns of behavior." In a monogamous relationship, with no point of comparison, you might think that all long-term relationships feel this way. When neither of you have gone on a first date in many years, you might forget how magical your relationship used to feel. Fern also shares a similar experience in her book *Polywise*: after years of asking her husband Dave to be a more proactive partner in kindling their romantic relationship, and to have him be kind and supportive but not passionate or romantic, something shifted when Dave started dating a new woman. "Suddenly *now* he has the skills and capability to create an experience *for her*, when I had just resigned myself to the idea that he was fundamentally incapable of doing so."

It is easy in monogamy to tell yourself, "That's just not important to me" or, "She's not wired like that" or, "All relationships simmer down like this over time" or, "I don't want to do that." It's important that, regardless of your relationship structure, you actively tend to making love an action in many different ways. Non-monogamy, in particular, forces you to pay attention to every aspect of your relationship and to be intentional about everything. It is much harder to imagine you've lost your sex drive entirely when you are hot for a new partner. It's hard to pretend your spouse isn't romantic when he's cooking a special meal for a third date with someone new. Regularly putting love into embodied action is a skill that monogamous people can learn and practice too, even if they don't have to. In an interview with me about polyamory and spirituality on the *Thereafter* podcast, co-host Meghan Crozier shared that she's already drawing on the wisdom of non-monogamy for her monogamous relationship. When she needs support navigating the complexities of (non-sexual, non-romantic) relationships in her life, or re-evaluating expectations and boundaries, she turns to her ethically non-monogamous friends "because one thing that I've learned is that in monogamous relationships, you never really have those conversations...I've learned so much about how to navigate and have conversations from my non-monogamous friends."[39] Meghan intuited what relationship researcher Ryan Witherspoon Ph.D. found in his study, *Exploring Minority Stress and Resilience in a Polyamorous Sample*: that the intentionality polyamorous and non-monogamous people bring to their lives and relationships translates into psychological and relational well-being. Witherspoon also noted in his study that "a growing body of research finds that CNM [consenual non monogamy] practitioners, including those identifying as polyamorous, report levels of individual well-being and romantic relationship satisfaction equal to, or sometimes higher than, monogamous controls."[40]

This commitment to love as an action translates into a faith context, too. As we practice love as an action in our relational lives, we strengthen that muscle and are better able to love outside the bonds of the people closest to us. As we practice love in action in our faith lives, we are reminded of the importance of loving our family and partners through actions and not just words. In the Christian scriptures, 1 John 3:18 says "Little children, let's not love with words or speech but with action and truth." The Torah is littered with injunctions to love, and it is just as clear that to love is to take action. When the Israelites were offered the Torah at Mount Sinai, they replied "We will do and we will hear" (Exodus 24:7). We will *do*, not just love or follow or believe. The prophet Micah lays out exactly what God requires: "to do justice and to love mercy and to walk humbly."[41] In Hinduism, the pain of life is seen to arise from a constant drive to control the world around us. We act to get or stop something and when we ultimately cannot control the universe, suffering arises. In contrast, when we are able to act out of a sense of pure love, we bypass this spinning wheel. We give out of love, with no expectation of transactional exchange. Here too, love is not just a feeling but an action. Krishna, speaking in the Bhagavad Gita (9:26), says, "Anyone who offers to Me with devotion, A leaf, a flower, a fruit, or a little water, That gift of love I accept, From one whose heart is pure." Actions are how you embody both love of others and also your faith commitments.

In progressive circles, faith and religion often have a bad reputation. Faith gets cast as silly superstition and religion as a controlling self-preserving institution. In my work as a spiritual practices coach at QueerTheology.com, I offer a reframe of both. Faith, religion, and spirituality are expressions and reminders of our deepest values. They are at times the embodied manifestations of what we believe and how we orient our lives, and at other times they are the inspiration we need to change our behavior to bring our actions in line with our values. Central to Judaism is the observance of *mitzvot*.

Drawn from the Torah and expanded by our sages, these *mitzvot*—sometimes translated as "commandments," other times as "sacred obligations"—are ways we embody in the world what it means to be a Jew. There is an echo of this in Christianity when the author of James writes, "Faith without works is dead."[42] Beliefs and ideals must be tied to actions to be meaningful.

Saying "I love you" to a partner, a friend, or your higher power is easy. Words cost nothing. How you respond when your partner wants something different from you, how you support a family member when they are sick, how you show up for your friends, if you are willing to take risks for justice, to sacrifice, to take care of strangers in need, that reveals the depth of your love. As you think about how to love well, I invite you to consider: What does love ask of you? What are you willing to risk for love? What does your love look like in practice?

Love boldly; it's worth it.

CHAPTER 5

Miracles

There is a story in the Tanakh featuring the prophet Elisha that, while about God's miraculous power, reminds me of the power of love and polyamory. In II Kings Chapter 4, Elisha has been traveling around performing miracles. In one place, he rescued a widow from creditors by pouring her single jug of oil out, filling up multiple empty vessels. She brought him all the empty vessels she could find and he kept pouring, and somehow the oil kept flowing until the last vessel had been filled. She was able to sell the multiplied oil and save her children from enslavement by the creditor. Later, he caused a barren couple to have a child, and years later, he brought that same child back from the dead. Later in the story, Elisha has just brought a child back to life, and has now returned to the town of Gilgal, which was being ravished by famine. There were, by this account, 100 people gathered when the man from Baal-shalishah arrived on the scene. Have you ever shown up to what you thought was a small dinner party with a small, delicately wrapped loaf of zucchini bread, only to discover it's actually a raging house party, with guests spilling into every room and out into the yard? I imagine this man felt something like that. Yet Elisha seems unconcerned, telling him to give out the bread and the grain and somehow, when it's all said and done, it's not only enough to feed 100 people, there is bread left over after everyone has had their fill!

Similar stories appear in the Christian Bible with Jesus feeding thousands of people. In the Gospel of Matthew, there are 4,000 people, five loaves, and two fish; in the Gospel of Mark, there are 5,000 people and seven loaves. In both versions of the story, somehow, after Jesus's followers distribute all of the food, and after everyone eats their fill, there are not only leftovers, but more food left over than they started with!

One way to look at the story of Jesus and the fish and loaves is that it's something that historically happened and that Matthew or Mark or both of them just got some of the details wrong. That is certainly the way many—but not all, or even most—Christians understand these stories. My view, and the view of many scholars, is that this story of Jesus feeding the crowd of thousands was developed to draw connections for Jesus's followers, all or most of whom were Jewish at this time, between Jesus and the prophet Elisha. It's a way of saying, "Jesus is like this prophet, but he's even more impressive." When the story of Jesus and the loaves was told to first century Jews, they would have immediately seen the connection between Jesus and Elisha and as a result, each would take on new meaning. In my work at QueerTheology.com, we teach a course called "Queering the Bible" where students learn to become sacred storytellers, looking at their own experiences, the values of their communities, and sacred texts such as the Bible, bringing them together to form a synergy that unlocks something deeper in them all. Drawing on ancient sacred stories can be a powerful way to make sense of the present. All of that is to say: you don't have to believe that any of these stories happened for them to be meaningful to you or for them to have something to teach you about your own life and relationships today. In the same way that Jesus's followers connected his life to their sacred scriptures, you too can connect your own life to the sacred stories you find meaningful.

Now, back to Elisha and Jesus and their multiplying loaves. One way to understand these stories is through divine, supernatural intervention. There was only so much food, but as the food was distributed, defying the laws of physics, the atoms in the food just spontaneously divided and multiplied and expanded and now there is more food than when the story started. Thanks be to God. That is certainly one way to look at it. There is another way though, that in my mind is just as miraculous. There are 100 people but the man and Elisha only have 20 loaves; there are 5,000 people but Jesus's inner circle only has seven loaves. But rather than send people away, the leaders in each story invite the crowd closer in: "We are in this together." Then, they start passing out what limited bread they do have. As they begin, someone in the crowd remembers the loaf of bread in his bag, or the three smoked fish she was carrying home from the market, or the bag of nuts they grabbed for the journey. Some people have a lot to contribute, some people have very little to add to the mix, and there are even some with nothing at all. Yet when it's all said and done, there wasn't just enough, there are leftovers! This is often the case in society: we think resources are scarcer than they are. In the United States, there are more vacant homes than there are people experiencing homelessness. In 2021, the United States produced 91 million tons of surplus food yet in that same year, 33.8 million Americans lived in food-insecure households.[43] We have more than enough; we just need to share it.

I'm partial to both interpretations of the stories and both ways of understanding the stories have a deep resonance with polyamory. Sometimes, like magically multiplying loaves of bread, love can simply expand. Every parent who has ever welcomed a second or third child knows this feeling well. You love your first child with all your heart, and then when there are two children, you manage to love them *both* with all your heart. One of my hobbies is running and cycling and as part of my training, I often take indoor cycling classes. At many of these classes, the lights are dimmed and the music is blaring. My favorite instructor Danielle Devine-Baum, who we lovingly called D.D.B., had just the right blend of technical guidance for an athletically challenging class mixed with a dash of inspirational woo. In one class over ten years ago that still sticks with me today, we were at a particularly challenging moment—a steep hill about three-quarters of the way through the class. We'd already been working hard and sweating harder. "For the next 60 seconds, I want you to give me everything you've got!" she cheered us on. I dug deep and gave it everything I had. Then, only 30 seconds later she said, "Okay, now give me just a little bit more for this last push!" Somehow, I dug deeper and found a little bit more to give. Sometimes, it seems as if you're already at the max—the oil in a jug, all the food, a full-on sprint, your whole heart—and then, somehow, there is still more to give. In this way, love is like a flame. When you use one flame to light another, the brightness of the first flame is not diminished; instead it spreads. Light enough candles and you can illuminate a whole room, or even a whole city. At first there seems to only be so much light or love and then, somehow, there is more.

If you look closely at a candle's flame as you hold it up to another candle to pass on the light, you might notice a brief moment when the flame flickers. It takes some energy to spark a fresh wick to light. In the exact moment that the second candle catches fire, a bit of energy from the first is used up to pass it on. After that, both candles burn just as bright. If you use a roaring fire to light a small candle, this energy transfer will not even be perceptible, but if you use a small, timid flame to try to light a big candle, you might see the flame briefly falter. If the initial flame is too fragile and the unlit wick too large or too dry, the flame might become extinguished all together. Love is powerful and love multiplies, but love is not invincible. You need to make sure that the flame of your love is well fueled.

These multiplication miracles for the expansive potential of love are beautiful, but there is nothing like your partner sleeping with someone else to bring you crashing down to reality. Polyamory is an ongoing, daily, sometimes minute-by-minute practice of putting your grand ideals about love into embodied reality. Is there really enough love to go around? Can you love without controlling? How do you love a person in the complete fullness of who they are? A year into my open relationship journey with my now-husband, he began pretty consistently seeing a new partner, Josh. In the beginning, compersion came easily to me. He was having a good time with this person; they seemed to have an easy chemistry. I enjoyed spending time with Josh, too, over dinner or drinks. As they continued to spend more and more time together, and their connection started to look more and more like "dating" or even "a relationship" as opposed to the "friends with benefits" with which it began, I noticed a jealousy brewing inside me. Josh and I lived just three avenues apart in Manhattan, and the Penn Station train station was about halfway between our apartments. Peter had been out of town visiting family and was arriving back late one evening. I had simply assumed he would come to my apartment to spend the night. I was just a few blocks from the train station and much closer than his home in Brooklyn. Though we never made explicit plans, he had done so many times before and so I never stopped to consider an alternative. At the time his train was scheduled to arrive, he texted to let me know he had made it safely back to the city and that he was popping over to Josh's apartment to spend the night. I was completely taken by surprise. The minutes after I got that text were some of the most uncomfortable I've ever felt in my relationship with Peter. I was spinning.

"Why is he choosing Josh over me?"

"We didn't talk about this!"

"Now that I think about it, he's spending an awful lot of time with Josh! What gives?!"

"They've been hanging out a lot without me. Why doesn't Josh like me? Why does Peter like someone who doesn't want to spend time with me? Isn't that some sort of red flag?!"

The rush of stories I was telling myself came hard and fast.

Some people in open relationships have a tool for just these types of moments: The Veto. If one partner objects to a connection—a person in general or a specific plan being made—they can "veto" it and the other partner has to cancel the plans or cut off the relationship. Most relationship coaches and couples therapists (myself included) are skeptical of "veto power" in a relationship as it can often cause resentment without addressing important underlying issues. My partner and I very explicitly did not have the option to "veto" someone but I am sure that if I had been able to veto Josh, I would have. With 15 years of perspective, that would have been the greatest mistake of my life. Josh became one of my best friends and the heart center of our chosen family. We've vacationed together, met each other's families, seen each other through heartbreak, illness, and incredible loss. How I reacted in the moments, days, and weeks after that text message from Peter is a reflection of the power of polyamory to force us to focus on love and commitment. Thankfully, I was not left to flounder alone that evening. I had a year's worth of research and study on the best practices of non-monogamy to lean on, translating all of my theory into practice. I also had a supportive network of friends to turn to. Some of these friends were also non-monogamous, while others were monogamous and had done the work to understand non-monogamy and had supported other polyamorous friends before me. I called one of my best friends while I gushed via text to two others. I paced around my room to expend some of the nervous energy that I could feel building. I called Peter to hear his voice, tell him I love him, and leave on a positive "have a good time!" note.

While my stomach was in knots and I wanted him to run to me, I also knew it was true that I loved him and I did, at least intellectually, want him to have a good time, even if that was with someone else. Then I went for a walk outside to get some fresh air. I stopped for a snack along the way. I came home and wrote in my journal. The next day, I reflected on what I was feeling, what the experience had brought up in me, and what I could learn from it. I learned that it's important to make explicit plans rather than assume I'll be able to see my partner whenever I want (I do not own him, after all). I learned that I wanted some more clarity about how Peter was relating to Josh, what he was wanting from that friendship, how we saw it progressing, and how he thought it might impact our relationship. I realized it had been a while since Peter and I had gone on a proper date and I wanted to do that again too.

It was through this experience that I realized jealousy can be an incredibly helpful tool. Jealousy is not helpful in the way it is often romanticized in our culture, as an indication of how deeply someone loves you; nor is it helpful when used for control or revenge. But jealousy does not have to be an emotion that you avoid at all costs, either. When you feel jealous, you can recognize it as a signpost that points the way toward an area in your life or relationship that needs greater attention. You can dig into that jealousy and follow it to see where it leads you. You might discover that you are feeling lonely, insecure, uncertain, confused, scared, vulnerable, or even just horny. Then the question goes from, "How do I make the feeling of jealousy go away at any cost?" to, "What do I need and how will I meet those needs?" Sometimes simply noticing and acknowledging your feelings is good enough. At other times, you might want to seek support from friends, family, or a partner. It is tempting to stop at jealousy, to let that awful feeling spiral and grow; to feel righteous indignation at how horrible jealousy is and how someone else has "caused" you to feel this way. Conversely, you might feel ashamed for feeling jealousy as if the presence of jealousy indicates some deficiency in your character (it does not).

If you feel those feelings or think those thoughts, that's okay. That is completely human. Try not to stop there. How can you transform your jealousy into a positive, actionable insight? What needs to change so that you can be more fully and more comfortably yourself? I don't always live up to this ideal practice of processing jealousy. Sometimes I sulk in my jealousy for longer than is helpful, but when I am able to dig myself out of the self-pity and take positive, values-aligned action informed by my jealousy, I strengthen the power of love for myself and for my partner. Love is not just a lofty ideal; it is a set of active, ongoing actions.

CHAPTER 6

Consent

B uzz... Buzz... I could hear the callbox on the wall by my door from the other room. It made my already pounding heart skip a beat. I gulped, walked to the doorway, and then hit the "Unlock" button on the callbox without even asking who it was. I already knew. At 26, and two years after opening up my relationship, I had finally worked up the courage for my first-ever kinky hookup, and now he was here.

In Genesis 32, Jacob is on his way to meet his elder twin brother, from whom he is currently estranged. The night before their tear-filled reunion, Jacob has a strange encounter that reminds me of that first kinky experience. Night has fallen and Jacob packs up the encampment where he, his family, and his servants have been staying. He sends everyone and everything across the river and stays behind. Alone, under cover of darkness, he lingers by the shore of the river. Maybe he's leaning against a tree or crouched in the bushes. Then, another man wanders up, a strange man he's never met before. Do they make eyes at each other? Nod their heads to beckon the other to come closer? They grab each other and begin wrestling. Their tussle continues, we are told, all through the night, "until daybreak"

(Genesis 32:24). The strange man presses his fingers against the socket of Jacob's hip—that is, he presses himself right above Jacob's groin. This all-night encounter left Jacob limping away, physically marked by the encounter with the strange man, who we later learn to be God.

That sounds rather similar to the stories many of my friends and clients have told me about their one-night stands: cruising in parks for strange men and all-night encounters that leave them limping a little the morning after.

I don't know what God the Stranger in Jacob's story looked like, but the Stranger in my story looked like a Greek god. He was tall, tanned, and muscular. Kinky hookups are an interesting dance. Often, one partner is "dominant" and the other "submissive" but those are roles we take on. My Stranger came to my living room and grabbed me forcefully, took the lead on our time together. Like God the Stranger in Genesis, he also pressed his fingers into the space near the socket of my hip and made me squirm. It was a match we both agreed to. I invited him in. I wanted him. We wanted each other. There is no indication in the story of Jacob wrestling with God the Stranger that it was an unwanted encounter, from either party. Why did Jacob stay behind after the rest of the party had gone ahead? Did he know God was coming? Did he arrange the meeting like so many sexual adventurers arrange for late-night rendezvous?

A few months after that first encounter with the Stranger, I met Andrew on an online dating and hookup site. We chatted for a few weeks before confirming plans to meet for yoga and a bite to eat afterwards. Much like Jacob met the man-God-angel while his family was away, my partner was away for the weekend the first time I met Andrew. He was sweet, charming, and adorable, with piercing blue eyes and dark brown hair. On our second meetup, we made our way back to my place. As we began peeling the clothes off of each other, we whispered what we wanted to do to each other—what we wanted to be done to us. Open communication is a pillar in kink communities. We talk about what we want to do, what we don't want to do, what we might want to try, how we'll let each other know if a limit is approaching or if we want a break. Movies like *50 Shades of Grey* portray kinky encounters as unexpected, chaotic, and overwhelming. They can be, but they're almost always carefully choreographed and discussed in advance. You know, at least vaguely, what you're getting yourself into.

The next morning, after Andrew left, I stumbled shirtless into the bathroom, my eyes squinting in the sunlight. As I came into focus in the mirror, I noticed a dark spot on my neck. A hickey. I took a step back to see more of myself in the bathroom mirror. I rotated my torso and hips and that's when I saw them: a few scratch marks across my side and a small bruise on my butt. I smiled. I hadn't set out to have a hookup that left me with visible markings after, but now that they were there, I reveled in them. They were signs of what I had been through, a reminder of the epic time I had had the night before with Andrew. Like Jacob, I was marked by my encounter with a stranger. When Jacob asks God the Stranger to bless him, God replies with a question. God asks Jacob what his name is. After Jacob answers, God says, "Your name will no longer be Jacob, but Israel, because you have struggled with God and with humans and have overcome." Jacob got his blessing. I wonder if Jacob thought about that night whenever he touched his hip joint, whenever his limp flared up, whenever someone asked him about it. Did a smile creep across his face, like it did mine?

In public discussions of polyamory, there is often an emphasis on love and commitment. Even in this book, we talked about love in the last chapter and we'll look at commitment in the next. When polyamorous people disclose their relationship structure, a question we are often asked is, "Is this about sex?" Our impulse is often to say no, this isn't about sex. It's about love and commitment. It's about multiple ongoing relationships, even as each of those relationships might look a bit different. "When you think of polyamory," we sometimes say, "don't think of an orgy, think of a shared Google Calendar and a lot of time managing logistics and emotions." That is all true. It is about love and commitment, but also, sometimes, it *is* about sex too. I want non-monogamous people to remember that there is value, even divinity, outside "long-term, romantic" relationships. Jacob's encounter with the man-angel-God-stranger lasted just a night, but he walked away with a blessing that would last a lifetime.

In the wake of the #MeToo movement—and similarly inspired movements within Christianity, Judaism, and other faith traditions—the conversation around consent has rightly seen a renewed focus. The Rape, Abuse and Incest National Network (RAINN) defines consent as "an agreement between participants to engage in sexual activity. Consent should be clearly and freely communicated."[44]

It is easy enough, I hope, to understand consent on the level of specific, individual encounters. I consented to the tussle with the Stranger, I consented to the scratches from Andrew. Polyamorous people are pioneers in inviting *everyone* to consider a consent framework for all parts of their lives and relationships. It is not enough for consent to start and end at the bedroom door, though. Polyamorous communities have long insisted that consent is required for *all* aspects of our relationships. Do I consent to be your boyfriend, girlfriend, or partner? What exactly does that mean? What exactly am I consenting to? Whether monogamous or non-monogamous, and no matter your religious orientation, this is a question worth asking of your partner(s) and also of your relationship with the divine. A non-monogamous approach to spirituality and to relationships requires that we put consent in the center of everything.

Eighteen months into my relationship with my now-husband, Peter, I started thinking about polyamory and open relationships. Since coming out, I'd met a number of LGBTQ+ people who were non-monogamous in some way. By that point, I had managed to shed my evangelical judgments that relationships needed to look the same way (married, monogamous, lifelong) for everyone, but it didn't occur to me that I might some day want an ethically non-monogamous relationship. Peter and I met on a now-defunct sort of LGBTQ+ social network. It was like a LGBTQ+ MySpace—complete with a wall and news articles—but you could connect with queers for friendship or flirting. We were friends for six months or so before we eventually began dating, and then a few months after that, "officially boyfriends." When we were 23, the distinction between "dating" and "boyfriends" felt *very* important. I suppose it was, because it meant, implicitly, that we were monogamous. To my memory, we never even discussed it; monogamy was part of the package that I asked for when I asked Peter, "Will you be my boyfriend?" By the time I was thinking about polyamory, we were each other's longest-lasting relationship.

When Peter and I decided to become "boyfriends," we adopted a set of default assumptions, among them that we would be monogamous, that we would see each other frequently, that we would talk daily, and that we would log out of our dating apps. There was also another set of assumptions that we seemed to agree to without ever making explicit: that our relationship was oriented toward living together, that we would get married (socially, if not legally, since gay marriage was not yet legal when we started dating), that we would take care of each other physically, emotionally, and financially.* There were some areas of our relationship structure that we did make explicit, though. We openly talked about finding other guys attractive still, even as we were committed to monogamy. We agreed that we enjoyed dancing with friends, and even strangers, when out at a gay club and that that fell within our definition of monogamy. We never

---

*This implied, expected progression of a relationship is called "the relationship escalator" and we'll go into more detail on that in a later chapter.

explicitly decided to be monogamous, though. We simply took that for granted. Years later, when I began seriously dating someone new, we took nothing for granted. It was his first time dating non-monogamously and my first time with a second serious partner. As we felt our relationship progressing beyond just casual dating, we felt "boyfriend" might be the right word to describe us. But what, exactly, does it mean to be a boyfriend? That was all on the table for us to decide together. We'll go into more specifics on the process of making and keeping commitments in the next chapter but I share this now to emphasize that in order to give consent, you must know what you are consenting to. Who and how you relate—whether to a partner, friend, divinity, or spiritual community—needs to begin with clear consent. Too often in both monogamy and religion, agreements are assumed and taken for granted rather than explicitly consented to.

Over the past decade, solo polyamorists and relationship anarchists have helped the wider non-monogamous community broaden the "defining the relationship" conversation to include *all* the relationships in our lives—friends, parents, co-workers, neighbors, and more—taking nothing for granted. This is another area where monogamous-minded people can pick up some polyamorous wisdom for their own relationships. I would propose that in order for a relationship to be ethical, it must have clear consent, and be free from coercion. That is a standard I apply to our own relationships with the divine, too. We should not tolerate from God what we would rightly call as abusive from a partner or parent. It feels important to ask, "What do I consent to in my relationship with the divine? What do I *not* consent to?"

There is a story in the Talmud, advanced by R. Avdimi b. Chama b. Chasa, that when God offered the covenant of Torah to the Israelites at Mount Sinai, God turned the mountain over and held it above their heads, threatening to bury them all under it if they refused. A Talmudic argument ensues, with R. Avdimi being aghast at such an implication, and going so far as to say that if true, then the Israelites and their descendants—all Jewish people, really—have a legal "out" from the covenant, since it was coerced. I'm with R. Avdimi on this one. Any relationship whether romantic, sexual, legal, or religious must be freely chosen and free from coercion to be ethical. This is sometimes easier said than done. When you care deeply about someone or something, it can be tempting to bend yourself to appease them. Where is the line between compromise and coercion? Between sacrifice and sabotage?

As a relationship coach, I specialize in working with individuals and couples who are considering non-monogamy or are in the early stages of opening up their relationship. When one partner brings up the idea of an open or polyamorous relationship, sometimes the other partner is already enthusiastically on board, but sometimes one partner is more hesitant or unsure. How you proceed when one partner wants something and the other person is undecided can become a mountain-over-your-head moment. I work with partners to slow their process down and avoid rushing to judgments or decisions. It may well be true that staying in a monogamous relationship would be untenable for you, but it is important for you to make sure you really mean that—that you are willing to accept the end of this relationship—and that you are not simply using the looming fear of the relationship ending to coerce your partner into a relationship structure that they do not want and cannot find a healthy way to engage with. For the hesitant partner, it's equally important to slow down and thoughtfully consider your response. Are you willing to accept the end of this relationship or are you hoping if you dig in to your position, your partner will acquiesce to monogamy? The question of consent in relationships goes beyond a simple "yes/no" of monogamy vs polyamory and can include all areas of how you build and structure your life together. These decisions will guide your relationship and you can think of all of them as sacred commitments too. The Israelite people accepted the Torah at Mount Sinai, so let your "yeses" in the life of your relationship be holy moments too.

It is worth asking what you agree to in your relationship with the divine. What assumptions have you simply taken for granted about who God is and how you "should" relate to them? I often work with people who do not see themselves as religious and yet it sometimes seems they are scared of a God they ostensibly don't believe in, judging themselves by a standard they don't value. They imagine that since they don't go to church, synagogue, or mosque, they are not religious. Sometimes they will tell me things they think they "should" be doing—things they don't seem particularly enthusiastic about. Even if they intellectually don't believe in God—or don't believe in a certain type of God—when the shit hits the fan, it can be easy to fall back into toxic ideas about who and how God is. "I must have done something to upset God/the universe/karma." "When the universe is good to me, she's really good. When she's bad though, she's really bad." Many of us have been told that who we are, how we love, or how we inhabit our body or gender is inherently disordered, that we are sick and disgusting. The Christian theologian John Calvin is famous for advancing a theology of "total depravity," that *everyone* is inherently worthless. There is a version of a God who is controlling, fickle, vindictive, and whom you have to walk on eggshells around, who could turn on you at a moment's notice, asks more of you than you want to give, makes you uncomfortable, and makes you feel bad about yourself. That God is an asshole and you are allowed to say "No" to that relationship.

Here is a good indication of whether God is a God worthy of your attention or a jerk who deserves to be kicked out: if your girlfriend, or husband, or dom wouldn't treat you like that, then God shouldn't either. In my work, I am committed to helping anyone who has felt alienated from their faith know that there is space for them and to reclaim it in a healthy and life-giving way. I'm equally committed to helping anyone who wants to walk away from a relationship with God and religion that isn't working do so fully and in a healthy way. Some relationships need to end. You cannot freely say "yes" to a relationship—with a person or with the divine—if you are not also able to say "no." If you want to say "no" to a particular way of relating to God, you'll learn some strategies for "breaking up with God" in Chapter 10. Whatever you decide about your relationship with the divine, it is your decision to make; there is no mountain looming over your head.

Attention to healthy boundaries has exploded over the past decade. According to Google Trends, there were basically no searches for the term "boundaries in a relationship" before 2011. Since then, interest in that topic has only continued to climb. In the "relationship advice" world, there is much attention placed on the distinction between boundaries and rules. The conventional wisdom goes that boundaries are limits you place on yourself, and guidelines on what you will accept and how you will react in certain circumstances, while rules are about trying to control someone else's behavior. While I generally agree with this distinction, I also agree with hosts of the *Multiamory* podcast that,[45] in practice, the distinction between rules, boundaries, and agreements is blurry and not always helpful. As more people hear "rules are about controlling other people" and understand that to be "bad," sometimes would-be rules will simply be restated as a boundary. An "agreement" is, in practice, usually a rule that two or more people have agreed on. It can be a way to have a relationship rule without saying you have one. A reduction of "boundary = good, rule = bad" keeps us from evaluating the different ways we give and seek consent in relationships on their own merits. And also, there are sometimes bad boundaries and good rules!

When two people in an existing relationship are deciding how to structure their non-monogamous relationship, it is common for them to set out a list of relationship rules. My video on "Open

Relationship Rules" is the most-watched relationship advice video on my channel. And for good reason! In my practice, I find that most often couples set rules for their relationship to protect the existing relationship. "We want to make sure our relationship stays most important," one client told me. That is an understandable, even good, impulse: to try to protect this thing you care about. While I work with clients in all stages of their open relationship journey from considering opening up, to newly open, through to long-term polyamory, most of my clients reach out to begin working together within the first two years of opening up their relationship. Many clients simply want to make sure they have a solid foundation for this new arrangement and are looking for some extra support. For clients who reach out six or more months into their open relationship, it's usually because something that *was* working has stopped working. I tell them, "Rules work really well...until they don't." Rules become unruly when they are imposed on someone who did not agree to them or when the relationship is not flexible and resilient enough to allow for all partners to grow and change over time, which might mean no longer agreeing to something they previously agreed to. Consent must be active and ongoing.

In the Torah, Genesis 12–25 tells the story of Abraham, one of the patriarchs of the Jewish people. In it, God has a special relationship with Abraham. They make a covenant—or commitment—together. The story of God and Abraham's relationship is told over years and chapters. They make promises to each other, they do favors on each other's behalf, sometimes they argue or get upset with each other. Though it is a relationship between a deity and a human, in many ways, it feels quite human. Then, in Chapter 22, God acts in a way that reminds me of a jealous, controlling love. "God put Abraham to the test," the text says. "Take your son, your favored one, Isaac, whom you love, and go to the land of Moriah, and offer him there as a burnt offering on one of the heights that I will point out to you."

When I read that, I hear in my head all of the people who have ever said to their partner, "Prove how much you love me."

Abraham takes his son Isaac and prepares to murder him to please this God. At the last moment, God intervenes and spares Isaac, providing a goat to be sacrificed instead. There is much debate among scholars, theologians, and everyday Jews and Christians about *why* God would make such a horrific ask of Abraham. The text is not clear on that but one thing *is* clear: Isaac's relationship with Abraham is never the same. There is a power and a beauty in making religious commitments, even ones that include sacrifice (we will get to both those topics in later chapters), but *you* must be the one making those commitments and sacrifices. It is unethical for someone else to impose commitments and sacrifices on you.

This can manifest in the world of non-monogamy through "couple privilege," where established couples, through their mindset, decisions, habits, and assumptions, center their existing relationship, even at others' expense, often without even realizing they are doing it because the culture around them expects and rewards that behavior.* When one partner in a relationship starts to date or hook up with someone new, couple privilege can show up as bad boundaries deployed in particularly harmful ways. I have seen this play out in my practice, and observed it among friends and members of various communities I'm part of. One couple who has been together for some time will open up their relationship and then decide, together, what any of their other relationships *must* look like. When one partner starts seeing someone new, that new person does not get to decide what they want their relationship to include or how it will progress; it has already been decided in advance, by someone who is not even part of it! When the new partner is excluded from discussions and

---

*This description of couple privilege is informed by Amy Gahran and her article "Stepping off the relationship escalator: Uncommon love and life." (see Chapter 10).

decisions about *his own relationship*, the situation is ripe for hurt feelings and ruptured relationships. When this happens, it reminds me of God and Abraham, conspiring together behind Isaac's back to decide things that don't just impact him—they harm him!

This dynamic can be present in monogamous relationships, too. Where couples decide together that certain people are off limits as friends for *both* of them or how much time one partner is "allowed" to spend with her family, to name a few examples I've seen. Of course, everyone is entitled to make decisions about what to do with their own bodies, how to spend their time, and how to structure their relationships. When those decisions are made with clear intentions, with everyone who is affected consulted and considered, and when each person takes ownership of the decisions they are making, *then* clear consent can be given. "I am choosing to prioritize my other partner over you and I am choosing to only see you once a month, on a date and time of his choosing, and I am not open to considering your feelings on the matter" *feels* icky to me personally, but at least it's honest.

In both your relationship with God and your relationship with others, it is important that consent—active, ongoing, clear consent—is always at the center of it.

CHAPTER 7

Commitment and Faithfulness

Human history is full of myths and metaphors to lionize our relationships with our spouses or long-time partners. Greek mythology says that originally humans contained two parts: they had two faces and four limbs. Some were two men, some were two women, some were a man and a woman. The gods grew fearful of these early creatures and so Zeus cut them in half, separating the two beings from each other. Osiris caused a storm to scatter the humans all over the earth. Ever since, we have been looking for our counterpart. We are looking for our one and only other half. There is a similar story in the creation account in Genesis, where one single human is created "both male and female" in the image of the divine. But this agender or multigender being is lonely, so God splits them in two. In modern Judaism, there is a concept of a *beshert*, the Yiddish word for "destiny" which has come to mean a soulmate. The formal belief is that your spouse was chosen for you by God in heaven before you were even born. Your time going on dates on earth is merely for you to find the one that is already destined for you.

The idea of a destined spouse isn't limited to the religious. Many of our romance metaphors reinforce the idea that there is one person uniquely suited for you and who fits together with you perfectly. The language of "other half" implies a person who is incomplete without their partner. That point is underscored in the romantic proclamation "You complete me." In this framework, we have to be with our partner. Who would want to go through life incomplete? And if you are the one who exactly fits together with me, then we have to stay together, because who else is there for me?! I agree with Jessica Fern that "The paradigm shift from the monogamous mindset of *I am with you because you are the only one for me* to the nonmonogamous view that *I am with you because you are special and unique, but not the only one*, can be difficult to grasp." I would take it a step further and say, "When I am with you not because you are the only one for me but rather because I choose you from a diversity of options—past, present, and future—it makes our relationship even more special. You're my one and only makes us a forgone conclusion. That there could be—and sometimes are—others for me and for you means we have an active, ongoing commitment."

Whether you are non-monogamous or monogamous, my hope for you is that you treat every relationship in your life not as destiny but as a choice you would make again and again.

How do you define "success" and "commitment"?

How would you define a success and commitment if your definition couldn't just rely on "staying together forever and never sleeping with anyone else"? This is a question I regularly ask my clients because "staying together forever" and "never sleeping with anyone else" seem to be our culture's markers for a successful and committed relationship. But do they actually deliver on their promises of a healthy, fulfilling relationship? It is entirely possible to imagine a relationship that meets those criteria but doesn't really *feel* successful or committed. In my work, many couples don't even have to imagine it; they are living it, and that is often what brings them to my digital door. Here are some ways I've seen that play out:

- A partner who is uninterested in your interests, concerns, or inner life.
- A partner who doesn't help around the house.
- A partner who works long hours and seems to care more about work than you.
- A partner who is completely uninterested in sexual intimacy with you.
- A partner who regularly prioritizes their hobbies over their family, leaving you to take care of the kids and run the household.

When I asked a sample of friends and clients—both monogamous and non-monogamous—the question, "How would you define success and commitment if you couldn't use 'staying together' forever and 'never sleeping with anyone else,'" here are some responses they came up with:

- "Healthy, communication, both personal and togetherness growth. Shared values."
- "Mutual respect and support, healthy communication, trust!"
- "To what degree you consistently will the good of the other person."
- "The amount of happiness you wish for the other in life, whether it includes you or not."
- "Few regrets about how you spend your time together."
- "More orgasms than bullshit."
- "Stretching comfort zone, joining in unfamiliar activities with genuine intent to enjoy."

- "Showing up (emotionally and physically) for things that are important to them."

These responses, while all very different, underline that the substance of relationship, not just the form, is key to experiencing it as successful. The form a relationship takes can also be important, but if you focus only or primarily on whether or not it is long-lasting or sex-with-other-people-free, you might end up in a relationship that looks from the outside to be thriving, but that is falling apart on the inside. As a relationship coach with a public digital presence, I sometimes get direct messages on social media from people in relationships who have seen me talking about sex and non-monogamy professionally but send personal messages wanting to flirt with me. I have been sent unsolicited nude photos from guys with "Happily taken by [their husband's username]" and whose Instagram feeds are *filled* with post after post of them smiling together in idyllic locations, with gushing romantic captions about how he's "the one and only." I've worked with clients who are seriously disappointed with the (lack of) sex life in their relationship, who are bored or frustrated, who fight often, who are considering breaking up, but who nonetheless have a "long-lasting" and "monogamous" relationship. We need a more holistic definition of success and commitment in *all* of our relationships and, frankly, in all areas of our life. When I work with clients, I encourage them to consider what *they* want out of the relationship. How *they* define success. What *they* are willing and able to commit to and what *they* would like their partners to commit to in return. Together, we make a "relationship roadmap"—which is just another way of saying a shared vision for the future—and then they begin to live this new vision together.

People of faith could use a "relationship tune up" too. Many of us have been spiritual for so long, and even part of a specific faith tradition for so long, that we might not be able to articulate exactly what "success" and "commitment" look like in our faith life. In the same way that some long-term couples are "going through the motions" long after the spark has faded, in my work as a spiritual practices coach, I see disillusioned progressive people of faith "going through the motions" in their faith relationships, too. They read the Bible or attend services regularly or put "Progressive Christian" or "Liberal Jew" in their social media bios. They react to the horrific news coming out of the religious right on their various platforms. That's all well and good. But what is your "ultimate concern"? For Paul Tillich, a German-American Christian and socialist philosopher, faith is the "state of being ultimately concerned."[46]

What is the substance of your relationship—with the divine, with your values, with religious communities of support and accountability? Here, an exercise that I and many other poly-competent providers use can be adapted to explore deep commitment and faithfulness in your romantic relationships, your platonic and familial relationships, and your faith life, too.

Commitment Clarity Checklist: For love and faith

LGBTQ+ people—monogamous or open—are more likely than our straight, cisgender counterparts to explicitly define what is and is not in the bounds of our agreements, particularly around monogamy. Of course, polyamorous and non-monogamous people are even more intentional and explicit about defining their relationship boundaries and commitments. Where you draw the "monogamy" or "cheating" line is highly individualized. In my work as a relationship coach, nearly every client is certain they are clear about exactly what counts as monogamy or cheating—and yet they are almost all different from one another. This differing idea on where "the line" is often includes people who are in a monogamous relationship together! One exercise

I walk clients through is the Commitment Clarity Checklist. This is an assessment of your understanding of what is inside or outside the bounds of your relationship agreement, *at this moment*. It is a tool to create more security and connection in a relationship, while opening the door for future possibility in a way that feels safe and committed, and includes defining activities such as:

- masturbating alone
- masturbating with another person present
- watching porn
- watching a porn livestream
- interacting with sexually charged social media posts
- exchanging sexually explicit direct messages with others
- dancing with a friend at a club
- dancing with a flirtatious stranger at a club
- kissing friends
- going to a nude beach
- being in a steam room where sex is happening
- logging into an online dating app but not messaging anyone
- talking on a dating/hookup app but not meeting up
- having long conversations about deep, vulnerable, emotional topics with someone who is not your family member or partner.

For each item above, I've had at least one client say that would be cheating and I've also had at least one client say it falls within the bounds of monogamy. This is why clarity is so important. You and your partner may have different understandings of what commitment means. It's not my job to be the sole arbiter of relationship boundaries—monogamous, polyamorous, or otherwise. It's not my job to define "the line" for every relationship. It *is* my job to make sure that all partners are on the same page and that they are giving their clear consent to all parts of the relationship.

If it is important to make clear commitments in a romantic re-lationship, how much more so is it to make explicit commitments to our higher power or deepest values? The 613 *mitzvot* in Judaism are a bit of an ancient Commitment Clarity Checklist, defining the Jewish people's commitments to ourselves, each other, and our higher power. Different movements among the Jewish people have different understandings of what these *mitzvot* mean, how we relate to them, and what is required of us; in much the same way that different people have different ideas about what romantic relationships mean, how we relate in them, and what is required of us. Many liberal and secular Jews understand the *mitzvot* to be a sort of sacred technology, developed by our ancestors and adapted throughout the generations as a means of cultivating a connection with the sacred, forming and protecting community, and transmitting our values. Much like my Commitment Clarity Checklist, many Jews define their own relation-ship to the various *mitzvot*. We take what works, adapt what needs adjusting, and set aside what no longer serves us. Orthodox com-munities take a stricter view of the *mitzvot*, understanding them as binding on *all* Jews; but even there, the collection of *halacha*, Jewish law, has defined, interpreted, expanded, and updated how Jews relate to our sacred obligations. There is varying interpretation between Orthodox communities, and even among individual Orthodox Jews there is some amount of personal application. Just as there are many different ways to live out a "committed" or even "monogamous" re-lationship, so too do different Jews live out their faith commitments.

While I speak here as a Jew, this process of defining and rede-fining our individual and communal faith commitments happens across all the world's major religions. Creeds and confessions are one way individuals make faith commitments—even if, for many people, the applicability of those ancient creeds to modern life is not clear. Inside the Soulful Sexuality course at QueerTheology.com, my cre-ative partner Fr. Shannon T.L. Kearns and I walk students through explicitly articulating their own sexual and relational ethics, as well as their Personal Action Framework: the interests and boundaries they are placing on their own sexual and relational decisions. Every faith tradition is, of course, unique but one thing all religious and spiritual traditions share is an evolution in their understanding of what commitment to God looks like. Even the most fundamentalist of religious sects engage in interpretation and adaptation.

In both my personal and professional life, I often hear from people who have some vague sense of spirituality or say that they miss some aspect of a former faith life, but that their lives, values, interests, and beliefs don't really align with what they imagine "being religious" looks like. "I should go to church more," "I miss the community and the singing, but I don't believe in a Sky Daddy anymore," "The Catholic Church was really important to my parents, but I don't agree with their stance on LGBTQ+ people," "Being Jewish means a lot to me, but I think Shabbat services aren't really my scene." In the same way that many people bundle together assumptions about what it means to be "in a relationship," they also bundle together assumptions about what it means to be "religious" in general or a specific religion in particular. "If I'm not monogamous, I can't really be in a loving, committed relationship" is false and so too is, "If I don't like any church service I've ever been to, I can't be a Christian."

You get to decide what your commitments look like in faith, family, love, and sex. In a healthy relationship, we explicitly define our expectations, ask for what we want and need, and adjust as circumstances change. In unhealthy relationships, we bring in unspoken assumptions, act passive aggressively, and tend toward conflict rather than collaboration. The same is true for healthy and unhealthy spiritual relationships—with the divine and with our communities of faith. Let's explore what spiritual folks of all stripes can take from the best practices of polyamory and other forms of non-monogamy when it comes to making and keeping commitments.

A spiritual smorgasbord: Deconstructing the DTR

Of course, it is not enough to simply define the boundaries of your relationship—to be clear on what is and is not cheating, or on how exactly you'll structure your open or polyamorous relationship—it's also important to make sure to have clarity on all aspects of how you will relate to one another. With a clear vision for your relationship, in the broadest sense of the word, you can work toward filling it up with exactly what is fulfilling to each of you. I first became aware of the power of defining each and every relationship on its own terms through the relationship anarchy community. Relationship anarchy is a form of polyamory where the people involved decide on what that structure of a relationship looks like. In relationship anarchy, you don't take anything for granted and intentionally choose and consent to each element of your relationship. The Relationship Anarchy Smorgasbord, originally developed by Lyrica Lawrence and Heather Orr of Vancouver Polyamory and expanded over the years by various members of polyamorous communities, presents a smattering of different elements that any given relationship could have. They're grouped together in circles by theme, almost like small plates that you might find at a feast. Together with any person in your life, you can use this tool to identify what, exactly, you would like your relationship to include. There are even spaces to add in elements that aren't included on the worksheet. True to the "you get to decide for yourself" ethos of polyamory, there are now countless versions of the Relationship Anarchy Smorgasbord, each designed for that person or that community's needs. Many polyamorous people don't even use a specific tool, but rather talk through with their partners how they want to relate to one another. The next page shows one page from the version I use with my clients.

This tool is not only for romantic relationships; you can use it for all types of relationships, including friends, roommates, co-workers,

	Your Name	Their Name	Notes
Social			
Meeting friends			
Meeting metamours (your partner's partners)			
Arriving at / leaving from social events together			
Meeting immediate family of origin			
Meeting extended family of origin			
Attending immediate family gatherings together			
Attending extended family gatherings together			
Emotional Intimacy			
Asking for / offering support in difficult times			
Sharing inner emotional world (thoughts, feelings, hopes, fears)			
Support in mental health struggle			
Sharing joy & happiness			
Saying "I love you"			
Being vulnerable			
Helping to meet each other's attachment needs			

A Deconstructed DTR   **Relation***shift*   relationshift.us

and neighbors. While non-monogamous folks are more likely to mix and match from across "plates"—for example, choosing "kissing," "kink," "going on dates," "shared accounts," and "partner" with multiple people—this tool is useful for monogamous people, too. You might only want to have one spouse, but you might decide "living together" is important for a best friend or a relative, too. You might decide to have a "boss-employee" relationship with someone you also live with (or you might decide you need to move out before entering into that particular power dynamic!). If you have a creative partner, it's worth considering if and how you will share finances. If you are monogamously minded and newly dating, this tool is useful to revisit as your relationship progresses so at all times you know, exactly, what your relationship includes and doesn't include. You may be monogamous but are you planning shared goals together? Co-mingling finances? Living together? Exchanging rings? With this exercise, you can decide "yes," "no," "maybe," "in the future," or any number of "let's discuss" type options.

The Commitment Clarity Checklist and the Relationship Anarchy Smorgasbord are some ways that polyamorous people have taken the monogamous milestone of defining the relationship (DTR) and expanded it to fit their more nuanced needs. Licensed clinical social worker Matt Lundquist[47] explains, "Often, it's seen as setting rules about sex and flirting, establishing monogamy, or setting shared terms for thoughtful, transparent non-monogamy, if that's something you desire." For many non-monogamous people, DTR isn't a one-time conversation but rather is a process we engage in and revisit regularly over the course of our relationships. Monogamous people can adopt the practice of checking in and re-DTR at regular intervals to ensure that you're both on the same page and that the relationship is serving you well. As we saw in the case of the Relationship Anarchy Smorgasbord, it's not just romantic relationships that deserve some intentional attention; you can define *all* of your relationships. I even propose applying that same frame to your faith and spirituality commitments.

DTR with the divine

If you have any interest in or participation with an organized religion or faith community, you have probably been asked by friends or co-workers, "So are you religious?" I am asked this almost every time my line of work comes up with someone new. As I am openly polyamorous, I am also often asked, "So how many partners do you have?" On dating and hookup apps, I'm often asked both of these questions in the same conversation! The answer to both is: it depends on how you define that. For most people, the titles of "girlfriend" or "partner" are pretty clearcut. You either are or you are not, right? In some senses, yes: you have a boyfriend, partner, or (in my case) spouse, if you decide to use those words to describe yourself. You are a religious person if you identify as such. Peel back the surface, though, and you'll find that all of those words come with sets of assumptions that vary from person to person. Does being religious mean you attend services regularly? For Jews, does it mean that you strictly observe Orthodox *halacha*? For Muslims, does it mean you pray five times daily and only eat *halal*? To be a religious Buddhist, do you have to be a member of a temple, or believe in the more supernatural elements of Buddhism? Or is a regular meditation practice enough? Do partners have to live together? Do boyfriends have to be monogamous? Do spouses have to be legally married? When it comes to commitment—in both relationships and spirituality—the popular polyamory tool, the Relationship Anarchy Smorgasbord, can be useful for people of all relationship structures and faith backgrounds.

The Commitment Clarity Checklist and deconstructed DTR can be adapted for the faith commitments you make. Whether you are very traditionally religious, "spiritual but not religious," "not really sure," or any point in between, it can be a powerful experience to explicitly and intentionally name and claim what you do believe, what your values are, and how you plan to live. Whenever you do something *only* because it is what is expected of you, because it's what everyone else is doing, or because it's what you think you "should" do—whether that's monogamy or the religion you were raised in—you risk resentments and insecurities and rob yourself of the personal investment and dynamism that comes from explicitly and proactively choosing something for yourself, even if that something is what you've always known. As you think through your own DTR With The Divine, here are some questions you might consider:

- What are your most important values?
- How do you live out your values in practice?
- What do you believe about God?
- What do you believe God is not?
- What group, idea, or ideal bigger than yourself do you feel drawn to?
- What does your higher power expect of you?
- What do you expect from your higher power?
- How important is it to be part of a spiritual community that shares your beliefs and/or values?
- What are some non-negotiables for that community?
- How does your faith affect what you eat?
- How will you spend money in values-aligned ways?
- Will you donate to organizations? Will you give directly to individuals in need?
- What holidays would you like to observe? How will you observe them?
- What forms of prayer, meditation, or mindfulness resonate with you? What will that practice look like for you?
- What other faith commitments do you want to make?

This list of questions is, of course, not exhaustive. You are invited to add your own questions and responses to the list as you consider what is most important to you. I'd like to encourage you to think about the positive attributes of faith, not only the restrictive ones. Many of us have experiences of religion based on restriction: don't smoke, don't have sex, don't eat pork, don't leave too much of your body uncovered. But faith can also help us toward freedom. What if your faith commitments included a commitment to leave relationships and communities that were taking advantage of you? To honor your body's desires? To trust your instincts?

While you may already have some ideas in mind as you are reading this chapter, putting pen to paper (or finger to keys) is an important part of clarifying your commitments. I always encourage my clients to explicitly write out their commitments. This is important for two main reasons: the first is that it forces you to decide *exactly* what you are committing to. When it's only in your head, you might hold multiple contradictory opinions without ever deciding between the two. You might have a vague idea of what you want but without the forcing factor of writing it down, you might never clarify it enough to act on it. Writing it down makes you decide on the exact words and phrases you use to describe your commitment. Often, my clients *think* they have made decisions around their commitments—in relationships or in faith—but when I make them write them down, they realize they don't know *exactly* what they were thinking. The second reason is that when you write your commitments down, you have a visible reminder of your decisions. You can look at it and remind yourself of what, exactly, you decided. Our brains are exceptionally good at solving problems and making decisions but pretty lousy at remembering things. Write it down so you can remind yourself often.[*]

Healthy commitments

In the last chapter, we looked at consent and healthy boundaries and in this chapter, I have emphasized the importance of intentionally and proactively choosing your commitments. Taken together, these ideals could be weaponized in support of a very self-centered way of relating to everyone else. This is both true and not true. For

---

[*] You can download a fillable DTR With The Divine worksheet at thisisbgm. com/bonuses

many of us, many of the commitments we make in our life could stand to be a little bit more self-centering. This is especially true for non-monogamous and polyamorous people—and anyone with any marginalized identity—as we are expected to make ourselves small and uncomfortable for the sake of those with more power over us.

A non-monogamous-inspired approach to intentionality and specificity in your commitments to other people is *not*, actually, about being comfortable all the time. It's not about extracting pleasure from your partners while offering nothing in return. It's not about "good vibes only" or a rejection of anything that makes you uncomfortable. Sometimes, being in an intimate relationship with someone is emotionally or even physically uncomfortable. Sometimes, we choose to make sacrifices both large and small for the sake of our partner or the sake of our relationship. Sometimes, there is a very real cost to the commitments we make to one another (we will explore that more in the next chapter).

When my now-husband and I were considering legal marriage, a wedding-type celebration, *and* a move across the country, we went to a couples therapist for a few months for some additional support and accountability in identifying our desires, making specific plans, and managing all the emotions that can swell up during big life decisions. As we were talking on our way to the subway after one session, Peter turned to me and said, "Ugh, that was exhausting. How do you actually *like* therapy?!" While I had got Peter interested in therapy, he had got me interested in running and so there was a perfect analogy here: sometimes when I am in the middle of a therapy session, it is uncomfortable. Sometimes making time for and getting to the session itself is inconvenient. Sometimes I have to take extra time to rest and repair afterwards. That's quite like training for a race. You put in some hard, uncomfortable, and inconvenient work before the race so that when race day comes, you're ready to sail through the course and across the finish line. Not only that, the work you put in has positive effects that spill over into your day-to-day life. The same is true with individual and couples therapy—or any work you do on yourself or your relationships—you are exerting some hard, uncomfortable, inconvenient energy now so that the rest of your life can run more smoothly.

Discomfort in our committed relationships does not only stem from this sort of self- and relationship-improvement work, though. Depending on your commitments, you might spend (or invest, depending on how you look at it) money to support your partner (or friend or roommate or business partner). The cost might be literal. There could be a social cost to asking for a "plus two" instead of just a plus one. Defending your wife against your parents when they say something sexist might be uncomfortable for you and for them. Choosing to take a pause from dating—or to put off starting a time-consuming hobby—with the arrival of a new child so that you can be an equitable co-parent might not be what your instinct is, but it might be what your commitment requires. You can never create a relationship without conflict, where everything is always easy. That should not be your goal. The trust, depth, and stability of long-term romantic and platonic relationships come from knowing deep in your gut that when push comes to shove you can count on each other. What is important is that you are clear about the commitments you make, that you enter them free from physical, mental, emotional, or spiritual coercion, that they are equitable, that they support everyone's individual agency, and that they contribute to the health of the relationship. Make commitments from a place of power and intention, and remember that you are always free to change your mind.

Expanding the scope

As you have seen in this chapter, polyamorous people take commitment seriously. Intentionally deciding who we are committing to and what, exactly, that commitment looks like is part of our approach to commitment that anyone can learn from and apply in their own lives. We also recognize that we can have multiple commitments and that a commitment to one person need not crowd out others in our life. You'll notice again and again in this book that I am inviting you to expand the scope of what is possible and who is included. Polyamory and almost all spiritual traditions ask us to expand our focus from a narrow focus on only ourselves and our immediate family (and in the case of monogamy, a focus on one and only one partner) to include a care for and even commitment to a wider community and higher cause. We will explore the emotional and theological implications of this breaking down of boundaries that both polyamory and faith can invite us into in a later chapter, but for now I'd like you to consider practical ways you might expand your understanding of "commitment" in ways that are aligned with your values.

Who else besides your romantic partner might you want to make some specific commitments to?
When reflecting on this question in my own life, I realized that living far away from my core queer chosen family was making it difficult for me to show up for them in the ways I would like to, so I moved back to the east coast to be closer to them. One of my best friends and I (along with my husband, of course) have been exploring what it might look like for us all to live together or at the very minimum how we will take care of each other as we age. Years ago, my then-pastor Reverend David Lewicki suggested that one way you can know if a person is your life partner is by considering the questions: "Who do I want to hold me as I die? Who do I want to be with as I die?" That framework spoke to me as it cuts right to the core of what it means to be human: to live and to love and to die. This somewhat morbid question dispenses with niceties and asks us to consider what is really important to us. At the time, I was almost a year into dating my

now-husband and when David posed that question, I knew immediately that "Peter" was the answer. With over a decade of polyamorous experience since I first heard that question, my answer has grown too. I'd include my sister and my parents on that list. Now, my best friend Matt is on it, as are the core of my queer chosen family. This isn't a hypothetical question for me, but one that I have lived. In 2021, one of my best friends died from cancer and I, and a few of our closest friends, were with him and his partner and his parents as he drifted out of consciousness. You can love your friends just as fiercely as you love your spouses. Your friends can even be a type of partner.

For people of faith, it feels important to expand our sense of commitment even further—not just from romantic partner to family and friends, but beyond that. I will reveal my bias here: it is my hope that as your faith and relational commitments grow, each one inspired by the other, you will find yourself needing to make solidarity with others part of your commitment, too. For Jews, the Torah is full of obligations we have toward others, including taking care of your neighbor and even taking care of the stranger residing among you. Christians are likewise called to "love your neighbor as yourself," while also being called to love their enemies. Taking care of the sick and the poor are obligations in Islam, too. The Quran (70:24) notes that giving to the poor is not charity but rather is giving "the rightful share of their wealth."

It seems to me that in many religious traditions, you cannot love God without loving both your neighbor and the strangers, without loving the poor and the sick and the widow. You cannot love God without concern for others. We are all bound up together. That boundedness is a commitment worth taking seriously.

CHAPTER 8

Risk, Vulnerability, and Sacrifice

I was a year into my first serious polyamorous relationship—the first time I had multiple, simultaneous, deep romantic relationships—when my then-boyfriend and I had a conversation that sticks with me to this day. "You've never gone through a devastating breakup. You don't know how vulnerable it feels to hold my heart open again, knowing it could be crushed all over again," he told me. Though I didn't fully appreciate it at the time, he was right. I'd been with my other partner since we were both 23 and things with him were still sailing smoothly. Sure, I'd gone through breakups, but they were only ever short-lived or when I was a teenager. The ending of a mature, long-term relationship was not something I had experienced. I have since then and he's absolutely right: it's crushing. The ending of a romantic relationship—or a deep, long-term friendship—can be incredibly painful. It is a death of sorts, the death of a future you imagined together, the death of the people you thought yourself and your partner to be. One of the reasons why loving can be so hard is because it opens you to the possibility of deep harm. Relationships involve risk. Even if you stay together with your partner for your entire lives, it is impossible for two (or more) people to live and love close to one another without occasionally bumping into each other. To be in a healthy, consensual relationship does not mean to be in a relationship free from any harm ever, but it does mean that each person involved is fully aware and explicitly on board.

While all relationships involve risk, the nature and structure of non-monogamy forces us to confront that reality. One of the core principles in Buddhism is the illusion, *maya*, of reality: that our perception of the way things are is *not really* the way things are. Monogamy offers some tempting illusions, too: your partner will never be attracted to anyone else; your partner will be with you for the rest of your life; your partner will love you more than anyone else; you are safe with your partner; you can count on your partner. The cultural myths around monogamy and coupledom, combined with legal, religious, and family support for monogamous couples make it easier for a monogamous relationship to seem less risky than it actually is. Of course, even in a monogamous relationship, your partner might find someone else attractive, they might leave you (or die young), might hurt you, might prioritize someone or something else over you (occasionally or consistently), might take you for granted, might be unreliable. Polyamorous people are not immune from illusions, either. We might imagine that because we have many partners, we'll be shielded from the pain of loss; or that since we have lots of relationship tools, our relationships will be more resilient; we might imagine we are better communicators or more thoughtful partners.

It is an uncomfortable reality that we all, whether monogamous or non-monogamous, must acknowledge: we cannot know the future and nothing is guaranteed. Buddhist teacher Pema Chodron[48] reminds readers in her book *How We Live Is How We Die*, "Whether we feel good or bad, our illusion of permanence leads to problems." This is why doing the work in the previous chapter of clarifying (and revising!) your commitments to one another is so important.

No matter how solid they feel, all relationships, by the nature of being composed of living autonomous humans, are constantly in flux, constantly growing, constantly changing. You can never remove the risk of pain or loss from a relationship, but by regularly paying attention to your partner and actively tending to your relationship, you can ride that wave of instability to deeper connection rather than be consumed by it.

Acknowledging that your partner might be attracted to other people—or even that your partner definitely *is* attracted to other people—can be scary. In most romantic relationships, the affection of our partner is wrapped up with a whole host of other practical and emotional needs: our sense of identity, stability, financial security, housing, sometimes even health insurance! If my partner is attracted to someone else, what does that *mean* about me and about us? I hear this all the time in my practice. One partner's attraction to another person is interpreted to mean something about the other partner. "I really like cookies and cream ice cream" says nothing about the inherent quality of mint chocolate chip ice cream, or even about what I think of it, and yet when one partner says, "I think that guy is really attractive," so many of us hear, "I think he's more attractive than you," "I don't value our relationship," "You are unfulfilling." For the record, mint chocolate chip ice cream (with rainbow sprinkles!) is my all-time favorite flavor of ice cream. But I do also really like cookies and cream.

Monogamy promises us that if we commit to it, it will protect us from those big scary feelings. Monogamy promises to protect us from risk, fear, jealousy, and vulnerability. "You are safe and secure now," it says. But does that work? I've talked to so many friends and clients in monogamous relationships who talk openly about how jealous and insecure they feel in their relationships. "I could never be polyamorous, I'm just too jealous," I hear on what feels like a weekly basis. Okay, well, monogamy doesn't seem to be solving that for you, now does it? Polyamory—and all types of ethical non-monogamy—is a practice of sitting with the scary unknown and trusting that you are enough, that your relationship is strong, that you are safe and secure.

As mentioned, I have been with my husband since we were both 23. I was his first "official" boyfriend and while I had a handful of boyfriends before him, none of them lasted more than a few months. We often wonder how our relationship would have played out if we'd never opened up. Would we still be together? How would we feel about each other? What would our relationship be like? Of course, there is no way to know for sure. We are not fortune tellers. I do have journals, though. And I know that in the early days of our relationship, in my early twenties, I had lots of questions about whether Peter was "the one." I wondered if we were the "right" fit for each other. I wondered if there was someone different or "better" that I was supposed to find. I worried that Peter would leave me. When we decided to open up our relationship, there was no pressing need. We were both incredibly happy in our relationship. We had a thriving sex life. Our communication and relationship maintenance skills were top notch (especially for guys in their early twenties!). As we discussed opening up over the course of nine months, we both regularly repeated that we didn't *need* to do this, that we wanted to take care of each other and didn't want each other to feel pressured. Opening up felt important to me, but not from a place of clawing desperation, rather from a place of stability and possibility. It felt deeply in line with my values of abundance, of collaboration rather than control, and of the good, strengthening kind of vulnerability.

Non-monogamy is an active and ongoing process in seeing, sitting with, and navigating the risk inherent in any intimate relationship. We release the story that this person *must* be with the other person and actively choose over and over again to stay with them and the relationship. This is, of course, true for any relationship, it's just that in a non-monogamous relationship, you are forced to confront that reality more regularly. I don't have to worry if Peter is attracted to other people; I know that he is. I don't have to worry if Peter wants to date other people; I have dropped him off on dates. I don't have to worry if Peter will fall in love with someone else; I have watched him fall head over heels. Through it all, I know that what we have is solid and strong. That's not some inherent quality of our relationship. It's not even enough that we continue to "choose" each other. Two partners can be miserable and yet continue to "choose" each other. Rather, this stability comes from continuing to stoke the fire of our love and commitment, even as we release control over the other person. There's a cliché proverb about love: "If you love someone, let them go. If they come back, they will be yours forever. If they don't, they were never yours to begin with." It's a cliché, but it's also true. I am no longer afraid when Peter goes on a first date, when he has hot sex, when he stays the night at someone else's place, because I have over a decade of practice sitting with that fear and vulnerability and over a decade of data that says yes, he's going to continue to keep choosing me, that I can trust him when he says, "I love you, I want to be with you" and I have enough trust in myself to know that, no matter what, I am already enough and I will be ok.

Non-monogamy reminds me of the practice of sitting meditation, which I first learned from Buddhist practitioners. In a sitting meditation, the goal is not to have no thoughts or specific thoughts or for anything to "happen," but rather for you to simply engage with yourself and the world as it is. It is a practice of releasing assumptions, distractions, and expectations and in doing so, allowing a natural calm to arise. The way meditation was explained to me by various teachers is that you sit firmly on the ground or a chair, you place your hands lightly on your legs, relax your gaze, and then relax your face and jaw. That is, before you begin, you must prepare. During a seated breathing meditation, you can use counting your breaths up to seven as a tool for focus, and then drop the counting as you get more experienced. This is an acknowledgement that sitting—with yourself, with uncertainty, with something new—is a skill that can be cultivated and that gets easier with time. During meditation, you may notice yourself thinking. That's okay, and is in fact part of the process. You can say, "thinking" silently to yourself and then return your focus to your breath. By noticing and acknowledging the thought, rather than willing yourself to ignore it, it is easier to let the thought pass you by. When you are sitting with the risk and uncertainty of your relationship, one tool is to notice and to name what you are thinking or feeling. This may be a literal feeling in your body ("my chest is tight") or it might be a symptom ("I am having trouble sleeping through the night recently"), or it may be a thought or story you are telling yourself ("I am worried you are going to leave me"). When we notice and name our thoughts and feelings, to ourselves and perhaps, if and when we are ready, to our partner, they become more discrete. They may still be scary or uncomfortable, but now they are not a looming shadow, they are something specific. When we have noticed and named the thought, feeling, or fear, we can begin to address it. A practice I use with my coaching clients is similar to the Buddhist practice of imagining your thoughts as being something outside your body (and perhaps I subconsciously adapted this exercise from my own experiences of sitting meditation).

It works like this: when there is a conflict, fear, or disagreement in your relationship that you are trying to resolve, you may be conditioned from our adversarial culture to think of this conflict as existing *between* you and your partner. It is as if you are standing on opposite sides of a high school gym playing tug-of-war. In order for you to feel safe and secure, you must pull your partner over to your side. You must convince them that you are right, that your feelings are valid, that your needs are responsible, and that they should give something up for you. Instead, try visualizing the conflict, fear, or disagreement as something that exists outside you both. You can imagine it floating in the air or set on a table or the floor. In your mind, place it not *between* you two but off to the *side*. I find it helpful to physically move your bodies so that you are side-by-side rather than facing each other. Sit on a couch or the floor, or scooch your chairs next to each other. Let your legs touch, or hold hands. You are on the same team and your conflict is *over there*. From a distance, you can look at it and make plans to resolve it, *together*.

Non-monogamous people practice assessing and managing risk twice over. The first, which we have just looked at, is how we confront risk daily in our relationships. We lay bare the uncertainty inherent in all relationships, we grapple with our partners' individuality and autonomy, and we collaborate to manage risk and keep each other safe and secure. The second type of risk non-monogamous people confront is the risk in disclosing to others the nature and structure of our relationships. Non-monogamous people form commitments in the face of intense risk, minimal social support, and nearly zero legal protections. One of the benefits LGBTQ+ non-monogamous people have is that most of us have early practice with assessing the we are and how we love and the risks we are willing to take.

When I realized that I might be gay, legal marriage for same gender couples was not an option—or even on the horizon—for any state. When I eventually came out, you could get married in just one U.S. state. As a teenager, I never thought that one day I would be able to get married legally to a husband, but that did not stop me from living true to who I know myself to be. I was not going to be discouraged from finding community, forming family, and yes, *getting married*. I would do that with or without the approval of a state or church. That was a sacrifice I was willing to make. So when I was in my mid-thirties and in a long-term relationship with two men and we were all considering options for our future, the lack of co-equal legal marriage available to all three of us was hardly a blip for me. I had long ago determined that I would find a way to make and keep family even without the government's permission, so that is what I would do now. We can find a way to make this work, I resolved.

When I work with straight, cisgender people who are new to non-monogamy, many of them are confronted for the first time with perils of risk and sacrifice that come with living outside the lines. What will my family think? What if my employer finds out? Can I still fit in my religious community? What are my marriage options, if that's something we desire?

In reflecting on her decision to publicly identify as polyamorous, Rabbi Nikki DeBlosi remembers what a rabbinic colleague shared with her: "You might have more opportunities to be hired at higher-paying institutions if you do not come out as polyamorous, you may be able to increase your *parnassah*, your livelihood/income, but in doing so you will decrease your *torah*, what you have to teach the world." Rabbi Nikki teared up as she told me, "That is too high a price." She was not willing to give up her *torah* for the sake of job security, so she began speaking about polyamory and Judaism from her personal experiences. There is no doubt that the Jewish world is richer for her courage. Not only do countless non-monogamous and polyamorous Jews look to her for inspiration and support, her unique experiences with polyamory bring a much-needed perspective to the traditions and institutions of her faith tradition.

Once you acknowledge the reality of instability in all relationships and have begun fitting your lives together, you will likely encounter times when it seems that one, some, or all of you need to readjust to make the pieces fit. Whether it's something as simple as scheduling conflicts or something much bigger such as differing expectations for the future, ways of expressing (or not expressing) emotions, or sexual interests, there will be times in any relationship where you are asked to compromise or sacrifice for the sake of your partner or the relationship. How do you know what is a healthy sacrifice versus an unhealthy one? The distinction is important because too many of us have had sacrifice weaponized against us by communities of faith, family members, and even intimate partners. Women are expected to sacrifice their careers for their husbands, LGBTQ+ people and polyamorous people are expected to sacrifice their comfort for their family's comfort, members of religious communities are sometimes pressured into giving more of their time or money than is sustainable.

A pattern I see often in my relationship coaching practice is that when partners begin to get serious, one or both of them will sacrifice their friends, interests, and sometimes even personalities for the sake of the relationship. Have you ever lost contact with friends when you or they enter a new relationship? Have you changed your eating, style, or hygiene habits for a partner? Have you taken on the vast majority of the responsibilities of running a household and tending to a relationship while your partner tends to his career, fitness goals, or video-game hobby? That's the price of relationships, we're told.

In talking with friends and clients who are single and actively dating, I hear stories of unhealthy and unproductive sacrifice all too often. Sexual dynamics that are unfulfilling or even sometimes actively unpleasurable, a lack of emotional intimacy, frequent fighting, a chronic lack of chemistry, a neglect of the little things to make you feel special, a wildly misaligned vision for life, and incompatible values are just some of the "sacrifices" and "compromises" I have seen people make for the sake of their relationship. As polyamorous and other ethical non-monogamous people, we are often expected to make "sacrifices" for the sake of those around us. We are expected to not talk about our relationships at work, because even the most banal life moments are considered "sexual," we're expected to only bring one partner—the partner we've been with the longest—to work and family functions, we are expected to be polite when people dump all of their relationship anxieties on to us when they learn we are non-monogamous. None of these are the sacrifices any of us should have to make. And yet we persevere.

There is an oft-quoted teaching of Jesus, where he tells his followers they must "take up their cross and follow me." It comes from three of the four Christian gospels, where Jesus is quoted as saying some variation of, "Whoever wants to be my disciple must deny themselves and take up their cross and follow me." This saying of Jesus has been weaponized against all sorts of vulnerable people as a means of coercing them to stay in unjust situations. It's said to women in unhappy or even abusive marriages, it's used to pressure LGBTQ+ people into celibacy, and transgender people into denying themselves life-giving transition options. It gets wielded to present sex-negativity as godly, and sexual and relational autonomy as sinful. Even more broadly, it has been used to suppress any sort of individual will in a person's life. It's also, frankly, bullshit.

A closer reading of the text reveals a very different, more revolutionary, message. In the context in which this teaching appears, Jesus has just asked his followers who people think he is and—more importantly—who his followers think he is. In each version of the story, Jesus's instruction to "take up your cross" is immediately preceded by one of Jesus's closest followers, Peter, making a treasonous political claim. In answer to Jesus's questions, his disciples offer a few different ideas until, eventually, Peter gets right to the point: "You are the Christ." In Matthew's version, the point is underscored even further: "You are the Christ, the Son of the living God." For the first time in the gospel story, Jesus's closest followers say out loud: "You are the messiah. You are the savior of the world." To modern readers, that might seem like a lofty theological claim, but in the context of first-century occupied Judea, it was treasonous. Living under occupation in the Roman Empire, Caesar was supposed to be the messiah. Caesar was the savior of the world. In 42 BCE, Julius Caesar officially became divine, taking the style "the divine Julius" (*divus*

Iulius) after his assassination. His adopted son, Octavian (later known as Augustus) thus became the son of God: *divi Iuli fillies* (son of the divine Julius) or simply *divi filius* (son of the god).[49] The Gospel of Luke explicitly puts Jesus in this context when describing the time of Jesus's birth with the line, "In those days, Caesar Augustus issued a decree..." In doing so, the gospel authors underline the competing claims of "God's son" which were not just theoretical religious beliefs, but treasonous political claims. And how did Rome deal with treason? Execution by crucifixion. Jesus's injunction to his followers about "taking up their cross" to follow him wasn't a lofty spiritual teaching, it was a very real warning: if you follow me in my mission, you will be executed for it. What are you willing to risk for your relationship? For the values you hold dear?

There are many times where risk and sacrifice might involve the risk of death. Certainly it did for the earliest followers of Jesus, as well as for many Black enslaved Americans fighting for their freedom, and for Buddhist monks protesting the Vietnam war, and countless other activists and organizers who, moved by their religious convictions or simply their values, were willing to risk and sacrifice much for the greater good. Though we may not think of it, there is an inherently religious connotation to the word "sacrifice" that is worth reconsidering in the context of both faith and relationships. Traditionally, a sacrifice is a portion of one's livestock and/or harvest set aside for God or the religious community. Sometimes the sacrifice would be burnt and destroyed, while other times it would be cooked on the fire and given over as a way to support the priests who run the temple. In either case, while the sacrifice was not insignificant, it was also not crippling and it was also in support of a greater good. A sacrifice—whether for your relationship or for your faith—should never be more than you can bear and should always lead to positive outcomes for everyone involved. If it is too great a burden—if it is more than you are *willing* to offer—and it does not support your relationship with your partner or the divine—we've moved out of consent and into coercion.

There are times when you may not only be *willing* to sacrifice but also *eager* to do so. You might willingly set aside some portion of your income to give to your community of faith so that the rent or mortgage can be paid, so that the lights can stay on, and so that your clergy can be supported. Your faith and values might inspire you to set aside money or goods for homeless people, single mothers, new immigrants, or other people in your area who could use some support. You might choose a small "sacrifice" by going with your partner's choice for dinner instead of your own, or skipping the game so your wife can have a girls' night with a visiting friend.

Healthy, long-lasting relationships always involve some amount of sacrifice and compromise. In my work as a relationship coach, I often support clients in parsing out which sorts of sacrifice and compromise are healthy for them, and which are not. It's critical that we are clear about who is sacrificing what.

CHAPTER 9
Ritual

I n the year 515 BCE, construction of the Second Temple in Jerusalem was completed and, with it, the Passover offering restored. Jews traveled from all over the land of Israel—or other places they had settled during their exile from the Land – and gathered in Jerusalem for this seven-day festival, bringing with them offerings and sacrifices. Before the sacrifice in the temple, pilgrims would fully immerse themselves in a ritual bath. There were prayers and blessings made by the priest, and after the sacrifice, a feast! The sacrifice became part of the meal.

With the destruction of the Second Temple and the expulsion of the Jews from the land of Israel by the Roman Empire, Passover sacrifices came to an end and were replaced with a seder meal, which Jews still observe today. It may be tempting to think about the sacrifice and later the seder as *the* Passover ritual, but a ritual is so much more than that. In the years that the Second Temple stood (and the First Temple, before it from the tenth to the sixth centuries BCE), the rituals of Passover began with the journey to Jerusalem, or to the temple grounds for those already living in Jerusalem. In fact, it began with the preparation for the pilgrimage. In the weeks leading up to Passover in the modern era, many Jews will begin eating up any *chametz* (food with leaven grain in it), and as Passover gets closer, some will box up or even give away or symbolically "sell" any remaining *chametz*.* On the evening before Passover begins, it is common today for many Jewish families to gather together after dark to search for *chametz* by candle light. A few pieces of bread are usually hidden around the house to make sure everyone can "find" and remove some final pieces of *chametz*. There are certainly religious elements to the Passover seder, but equally meaningful are the preparing, the searching, and, of course, the gathering together of friends and family for shared meals. Eating Matzo Ball Soup, made with the same loving recipe year after year, can be just as much a ritual as the seder or the Temple sacrifice itself.

Every religion and faith tradition has defining rituals. Some are explicitly prescribed by that group's central documents or key leaders, while others are created organically or adopted informally but are no less real and meaningful parts of the ritual. Many Christians eat lamb at Easter, which started as a nod to the Jewish Passover sacrifice that Easter replaced in Christianity. But many Christians eat lamb at Easter because that's what their parents made, and their parents before them, and theirs before them. Making a pilgrimage to Mecca is a central ritual within Islam, while reciting mantras is a ritual in Hinduism, and powwows are rituals in many North American native communities.

But rituals are not just for the religious (or maybe we're all a bit more religious than we imagine). Take one of the staples of the polyamorous community: Poly Cocktails. The first-ever Poly Cocktails was started in New York City by O Man, Diva, and Diana Adams, three polyamorous friends and activists.[50] It is a monthly mixer to

---

*After Passover, the food that was symbolically sold to a non-Jew is then "bought" back at the exact same price so that no food is wasted and there is no economic hardship for anyone.

bring together polyamorous people in a given city for informal socializing. It filled an important gap between more structured polyamorous spaces like conferences and workshops and more sexually charged spaces like play parties. Since its founding in 2007, Poly Cocktail gatherings have spread, informally, to dozens of cities across the United States on both coasts and in all points in between: Los Angeles, California; New York; Denver, Colorado; Madison, Wisconsin; Schenectady, New York; Houston, Texas; Austin, Texas; Chicago, Illinois; and more. Poly Cocktails are a core ritual of polyamorous communities: they happen at specific intervals, in specific locations, and there are specific expectations for attendees.

For many religious people, attending a weekly religious gathering is one of the primary ways to meet new friends and form community when moving to a new city—or when entering for the first time or re-engaging with that faith community. The same is often true for polyamorous and poly-curious people with Poly Cocktails. In Judaism, we have a holiday every single month: Rosh Chodesh marks the new moon and the start of a new (lunar) month. In 2017, the *Multiamory* podcast developed a framework for a monthly relationship check-in which is called the Relationship RADAR. Since then, tens of thousands of polyamorous people around the world have adopted the process. I'd like to propose that events like Poly Cocktails and tools like the relationship RADAR have all the elements of religious ritual. I'll share what those are—and how you can develop your own meaningful relationship rituals in just a moment—but first, I'd like to address an important question: why.

A habit or routine is any action or set of actions you complete regularly, whereas a ritual is more than that. A ritual is an action or set of actions that are imbued with a deeper meaning and when done repeatedly deepen your connection with yourself, your values, your community, and your higher power or purpose. Let's look at the relationship RADAR. The first step of a RADAR is to schedule the next month's meeting. This means that you always have at least one RADAR scheduled on your calendar at any given moment. This seemingly simple logistical consideration has a profound psychological impact: you are the type of person who is *continually* investing in your relationship and who is *actively* making it a priority. You could just set aside time for a "relationship check-in" or maybe even informally but somewhat regularly talk with your partner about the status and concerns of your relationship, but instead you've given it a *name* and set aside a *time* for it. Almost all religious traditions recognize the significance of names and the power that comes with naming. *Naming* your relationship check-in is a signal that *this matters*. It's not just any name and it's not just any check-in though. When individuals, couples, and other types of relationships sit down together to do a RADAR, they are joining with thousands of other people who are also doing a RADAR that month. We are part of a wider community with at least somewhat overlapping values and a vision for how relationships can thrive. The RADAR connects you to your values and even to a sense of purpose. There are the values inherent in doing a RADAR: commitment, open communication, honesty, collaboration, and accountability are a few. And then there are the values specific to you that you will focus on your particular RADAR. You might have a section dedicated to travel and adventure, or savings and security. Much like prayers and blessings ask us to reflect on our values and priorities, so too does the process of going through a relationship RADAR.

Of course, not every polyamorous person goes to Poly Cocktails or does a monthly relationship RADAR. But many of us have formed our own community, relational, and individual rituals to support, inspire, and sustain us, even if we don't always recognize them as such. For example, every Tuesday after work, my partner and I go for a walk around the neighborhood. We leave our phones at home, hold hands, and venture out at least around the block. Then we come home and make fresh tacos together. It's blocked off in our calendars as "Taco Tuesdays" and when friends or co-workers ask if one or both of us can get together during the week, Tuesdays are off limits (some exceptions apply, of course). It's got to the point now where all of our friends know about our Taco Tuesday ritual, and some have even started one for themselves. While I'm partial to Taco Tuesday, I've also seen Wok Wednesdays, Pizza Fridays, and Sexy Saturdays. The latter isn't even food themed; they just never make plans before 2pm on Saturdays so they can spend all morning in bed together (and part of the afternoon, if desired).

How do you transform a routine into a ritual?

In my work as co-founder and director of Spiritual Practices at QueerTheology.com, I identified seven elements to transform a routine into a ritual:

1. Time
2. Place
3. Order
4. Intention
5. Others
6. Integration
7. Repetition.

Let's dive into each element in more detail so that you can understand what is needed to build your own life- and relationship-supporting rituals. Then you're invited to turn some of your existing habits and routines into rituals—I hope you'll be inspired to create some brand-new rituals for yourself and the people you care about.

Time
One of the most powerful ways you can transform a simple routine into a powerful ritual is by committing to a set time. Different

routines in your life are likely already to have a set cadence and so your first step is to notice what you're already doing, and then perhaps be a bit more intentional about keeping to that schedule. For the grocery plan you and your partner usually make at some point over the course of the week, set aside 30 minutes every Saturday morning for a weekly Sync Session. The dinner you and your extended polypod have every now and then, could you turn that into a monthly tradition? The play party you and your friends threw that was a big hit, what if you tried making that a quarterly occurrence, complete with a seasonal theme?

While the above examples involve other people (we'll get to the importance of involving others in just a few sections), you can also transform personal routines into deeply meaningful rituals by picking a specific time. Meditating in the morning, journaling before bed, and knitting a special item are all routines that my clients have turned into rituals. By selecting and sticking to a specific time for a ritual, you give it a sense of gravitas. Shabbat happens every Saturday, solstice celebrations happen twice a year, Christmas happens every December. Your relationship rituals don't need to—and maybe shouldn't—follow the business calendar that the rest of our lives are often bound to. Islam follows a lunar calendar, which is about 11 days shorter than the Gregorian one, so the holidays, which are set on the lunar calendar, change dates on the secular calendar each year and over time float all throughout the Gregorian year. It has its own rhythm. You, too, can have rituals that follow a cadence that is different from your day-to-day life. You might have rituals that follow the school year, a sports season, or even your menstrual cycle.

Place

While some rituals you can take with you (I try to meditate daily even when I'm traveling), there is power in anchoring a ritual to a specific place. You might have your monthly Shift Sessions on a blanket in a nearby park during warm weather and at your kitchen table over a cup of hot tea in the cooler months. I have a meditation cushion I sit on (just about) every time I meditate. To help transform your routine into a ritual, change the physical space in which the routine-turned-ritual happens. If you want to have a ritual for coming together to connect sexually with your partner, you might turn on some colored lights (or throw a scarf over the lamp), light some candles, play some music. Of course, relationship rituals don't have to have the trappings of romance. You could also put on some slutty underwear, bust out some fetish gear, or use a white noise machine to muffle the sounds you'll be making. The important point is not exactly where you go or how you transform your space, only that you do it with intention and that whenever possible, you have your ritual in the same place each time.

Order

Jews all over the world pray the same prayers, in the same order, every day. While there are some minor variations between communities and on special holidays, in general, the order is the same day in and day out. We use a prayer book called a *siddur*, which literally means "order," to go through the motions every day. This practice of following a set order for religious rituals is, of course, not unique to the Jewish people. A Catholic mass has the same structure every Sunday; most yoga practices start and end the same way. There is something in particular to learn from the five-times-daily *salah* prayer in Islam. While there is a set order to the prayers, the order extends beyond what you think or say to what you wear and how you prepare your space and move your body. Incorporate your physical self and your space into the order of your ritual. One of the reasons the seventh inning stretch in baseball and the theme song of a TV show are so meaningful is because we humans respond well to order. Following a recognizable order is key to transforming your routine into a ritual.

Intention

The first step in *salah* is *niyyah*, which means intention. This ritual always begins with an intention. It's not enough to simply do the same thing over and over again. I brush my teeth and take my medicine every morning; that doesn't make it a ritual. However, I have clients who have transformed taking their medication—from anti-depressants to gender-affirming hormones—into a meaningful ritual. Playing video games with your partner could be something you do just out of habit, but with an intention to make it a ritual that connects you two over a shared interest, it can become a meaningful ritual.

It's really as simple as deciding "I intend this to be a ritual." If you want to solidify your intention a bit more, you could write a short sentence for each of these seven steps to have a physical representation of your intention. You could also add it to your calendar or to-do list, or set a recurring alarm. Talking about your ritual(s) with your friends and why it's meaningful to you—in the same way you talk about your other hobbies—can also help to solidify your intention. All of my friends know not only that I eat tacos every Tuesday, but that Taco Tuesday is an intentional and meaningful part of my relationship with Peter. There's a reason we do it.

Others

A routine that you do completely by yourself, for yourself, and disconnected from anyone else is going to be difficult to transform into a meaningful ritual. Part of what makes rituals powerful is that they help to connect us to others. Humans are deeply social creatures. It's wired into our DNA through hundreds of thousands of years of evolution, and captured poetically in sacred stories like Genesis 2 where God notices "It is not good for the Human to be alone." You do not have to be physically present with others in order to incorporate "others" into your routine. You might be physically alone in your home while you read the Bible or *The Ethical Slut*, but in doing so, you are part of a great multitude of other polyamorous people who have read that same book and seen themselves reflected on its pages. You can pray the daily prayers in most religions alone or with others, but even when you are alone, you are connected to all the other people observing that same ritual. Still, I recommend to clients and community members to have *some* routines that do physically involve other people. A monthly dinner with your extended polycule, an annual vacation with your best friends, a weekly meal at home with your partner. Do something together with people you care about and call it sacred. It is.

Integration

The impact of your rituals can—and should—extend beyond the time when you are actively involved in them. Rituals have the power to transform our whole lives. In some ways, they are play-acting our vision for the future. My chosen family's trips to Fire Island are meaningful while we are there, but they also infuse our lives off the island too. We leave refreshed, restored, and reconnected. More than that, on the island we get a glimpse of what the world could be like: where LGBTQ+ people are fully safe and fully comfortable expressing themselves openly, where time moves more slowly, where we are less connected to our phones and more connected to each other. Couples who have a monthly check-in ritual will feel more connected and aligned in the moment, but the effect of that ritual ripples out throughout the month. The decisions you make during the check-in will play out over the coming month, and more than that you will know that you are the type of couple who makes tending to your relationship a priority. As you begin transforming routines into rituals—and starting brand-new rituals—pay attention to how you might integrate those experiences into your larger life.

Repetition

An experience you do just once might be deeply meaningful, but it's not (usually) a ritual. The final step in transforming a routine into a ritual is to do your rituals over and over again, on the appropriate timeline. As you repeat your ritual over and over again, it will take on new and deeper meaning. The first time I went on vacation with my best friends to Fire Island, it was an exciting adventure. Now, ten years after that first trip, it is a deeply meaningful ritual for us. When you start a new ritual, it may not be as meaningful as other rituals you used to have. That makes sense; it doesn't have years of patina to give it character. So don't abandon a ritual just because it isn't deep and transformative right away. Often, the real power builds over time. When we began our annual Fire Island vacation tradition, we had no idea that six years later, we would trade late night drinks and dancing in our underwear for sitting poolside with the heartbeat of our friend group who was now too sick to walk down to the beach. Or that, in the years since his passing, those boardwalks would remind us of all the carefree memories we shared together before cancer took him from us. Every time you do your ritual, you meet the new moment and you also bring with you all the memories of the past. In a ritual repeated, you suspend the rules of time and merge past, present, and future into one powerful moment.

Put the seven elements together and define your own rituals

Now that you know the seven elements of a ritual, it's time to start crafting some of your own! Some might be more focused on strengthening particular relationships while others might be focused on deepening your spirituality, but as you've just seen, all rituals connect you to both others and that-which-is-bigger-than-yourself. Start first by identifying any obvious rituals that you already have such as going to religious services. Do these serve you? Are there any elements of it that could be strengthened? (In my experience, a specific Intention, connection to Others, and Integration into your life outside the ritual are often strong candidates for a bit of extra attention.)

Next, turn your attention to any routines and other regular or semi-regular activities in your life. Are any of these good candidates for transformation from a simple routine into a more meaningful ritual? Vacations, clubs, game nights, and the go-to grooves you may have fallen into with your partner are all things to consider. Do you have a favorite take-out spot you often order from with your partner or roommate? Do you rewatch the same movie every year? Do you somewhat regularly invite folks over for dinner? These types of activities in your life are prime candidates for transformation into ritual. Consider the communal actions you're already taking and focus in on the ones that you enjoy the most. What is it about them that you appreciate? Go through each of the seven elements of a ritual and find ways to intentionally craft each of them just a little bit.

As you begin turning a few of your routines into rituals, you may notice that you don't actually have many routines or that the ones you do aren't particularly meaningful to you. That's okay! This is also a moment for you to thoughtfully consider what rituals you would like to proactively create to strengthen your spirituality and your relationships. As you brainstorm the routines you'd like to add—and the elements you'll add to each existing routine—be mindful as to how these can reflect and strengthen your values and your understanding of a higher power. If hospitality is an important value to you, consider a ritual centered around hosting people. If adventure is a value, consider a monthly ritual (with friends and/or partners) that takes you outside your comfort zone. If justice is a value, consider how you might regularly work with others to make your community more equitable. *Voila!* You've got a handful of rituals to support your spirituality and your relationships of all sorts!

Psychotherapist and polyamorous relationship expert Jessica Fern developed a six-part framework for the elements required in secure relationships. The fourth one, "Rituals and Routines", expresses what I've also discovered in both my personal life and relationship coaching practice (no doubt informed by my work as a religious educator as well): that relationship rituals are not only fun and meaningful in the moment, they are critical to the long-term success of a relationship and their benefits spill over into your life and relationship long after the activity is over. Humans crave the consistency and predictability of patterns and so when you and your partner or partners do the same things over and over again, you send deeply comforting signals to yourself that you can count on this person and this relationship.

The benefits of relationship rituals are especially important for preventing or addressing stress or conflict in a relationship. As you saw in the chapter on love, small, repeated actions are a powerful way to put love into action. There is value to these actions in and of themselves, but their potential is multiplied when you recognize them as relationship rituals and intentionally infuse them with extra meaning. For instance, the short phone-free, hand-holding walk I suggested in Chapter 4? That has multiple psychical, emotional, and psychological benefits all on its own. The act of holding hands is an embodiment of your commitment and connection. Putting away screens, holding hands, being outside, and being able to look further into the distance are all somatic interventions. Doing them together has the additional benefit of helping you and your partner co-regulate each other. All that happens without you even having to think (or talk!) about it. But, there's more! When you combine that simple action with the seven steps to transform a routine into a ritual, you supercharge the positive effect on your relationship. Your simple routines become important rituals. They become something you are doing, in a special way, to deepen your commitment to others.

What Jessica Fern and the *Multiamory* podcast hosts seem to grasp instinctively, I'd like to make explicit: transforming simple habits into meaningful rituals supercharges the effect they have on you and your relationship by connecting those activities to your deeper values and your wider community.

For all the anxiety that can go into holiday celebrations, there is also a tremendous amount of joy. Take Christmas. You know exactly when it will be: December 25. You spend weeks or months preparing for it by buying presents, decorating your house, and planning meals. Maybe there is a last-minute rush of excitement or dread as the day gets closer. "How will my family act this year? Will I get that one gift I really want?" Planning and preparing for the holiday is part of the fun. It adds to the excitement and makes it that much more special.

When two people are in a relationship for a long time—whether they are monogamous, open, or polyamorous—it is natural for them to settle into some predictable habits and rhythms. This is not only completely normal, it's also a *good* thing. The anxious unpredictability of new love which turns your world upside down is exciting, but you can only sustain it for so long. Familiar habits that you form together with your partner, like which side of the bed you sleep on, pet names you call each other, and your favorite go-to meals, all serve to psychologically reinforce the stability of your relationship. Relationship rituals help you to work *with* this stability, rather than against it. While the familiarity of a stable, long-term relationship can lead to a decrease in erotic desire, intentionally making relationship rituals is one way you can continue to infuse romance, adventure, and exploration into your relationship.

When clients or community members come to me and want to integrate their spirituality with their relationship structure, their first impulse is to want to "do" spiritual things with their partners. They will often express, "I wish my partner would go to services with me," "I'd like to work through a Bible study with all my partners together,"

"It would be really nice if she would pray with me." Doing tradition-ally spiritual or religious activities with your partner or partners is certainly one way to integrate your queerness and/or polyamory: by acting out these religious activities, you are literally—with your body—bringing polyamory and spirituality together. But simply adopting traditional religious habits like services, prayer, Bible study, or overt theological discussions is not the only way to integrate poly-amory and spirituality. In fact, in my experience, it is one of the more superficial types of integration. What if polyamory and spirituality were so integrated for you that they became fused? That it became almost impossible to say where one ends and the other begins? What if every part of your polyamory was already spiritually significant— the highs and lows of a relationship like wedding celebrations and mourning the passing of a partner, of course, but also the boring everyday work it takes to keep your relationship humming along? And as most every polyamorous person knows, healthy relationships involve a lot of logistics!

As you have seen and will continue to see throughout this book, the practice of non-monogamy is a about paying attention to yourself and to others. That in and of itself is a holy act. It is important to remember that God is not somewhere else outside yourself and your daily lives—at church, in a Torah study, at a prayer meeting. God is there, but God is also in the way you care for your community and make love to your partner and celebrate silliness. Rituals help you to notice and name as holy diverse parts of your life and the human experience and in doing so, you paint a more beautiful picture of the divine.

CHAPTER 10

Loss and Grief

I n Chapter 1, I shared the story of author Colin Wright's "breakup party" and while (as far as I know) he is straight and monogamous, Colin and his then-girlfriend were clued into a truth that many polyamorous people know and that is scandalous to many monogamous people: breakups don't need to be seen as failures. There are two truths that I hold at the same time: it is true that a breakup or divorce does not need to be seen as a failure or loss and it is also true that sometimes breakups and divorces absolutely do feel like incredible losses. Polyamorous and spiritual communities have both developed practices around "endings"—practices for ending relationships and practices for the end of life. In this chapter, we'll explore how a polyamorous approach to ending relationships could be useful for monogamous relationships as well and then we'll look at how some spiritual practices might be adapted to support and soothe us through painful relationship losses.

In polyamorous communities, we've created a whole new word to replace "breakup;" instead many polyamorous people talk of "de-escalating" their relationship. In 2012, Amy Gahran coined the term "relationship escalator" in an article on her blog, *Solo Polyamoy*. The "relationship escalator" is the set of assumptions that modern culture places on romantic relationships. She even identified a specific order in which those relationship stages are assumed to play out. If a relationship is "serious," culture expects it to follow a certain path. Here are the stages Gahran identified, as described in her book *Stepping Off the Relationship Escalator:*[51]

1. *Making contact:* Flirting, casual/occasional dates, and possibly sex.
2. *Initiation:* Romantic courtship gestures or rituals, emotional investment ("falling in love"), and almost certainly sexual contact, except for religiously or socially conservative people.
3. *Claiming and defining:* Mutual declarations of love, presenting in public as a couple (becoming an "us"), adopting and using common relationship role labels ("my boyfriend," etc.). Having expectations, or making explicit agreements, for sexual and romantic exclusivity—and also ending other intimate relationships, if any. Transitioning to unbarriered vaginal/anal intercourse, if applicable, except if that would present unwanted pregnancy risk. Once this step is reached, any further step, including simply remaining in the relationship, can be considered an implied commitment toward intentions of a shared future.
4. *Establishment:* Adapting the rhythms of your life to accommodate each other on an ongoing basis. Settling into patterns for spending time together (regular date nights and sexual encounters, spending time in each other's homes, etc.), and communicating (speaking, phoning, or texting when not together, etc.).
5. *Commitment:* Discussing, or planning for, a long-term shared future as a monogamous couple. Expectations of mutual accountability for whereabouts and behavior. Meeting each other's family of origin.

6. *Conclusion:* Getting legally married. Having children, which is no longer viewed as mandatory, but still strongly socially venerated. The relationship is now "finalized" and its structure is expected to remain static until one partner dies.

7. *Legacy:* Purchasing a home together, raising a family together. These are no longer universally viewed as mandatory, but often a couple may not feel or be treated as fully "valid" until they hit these post-marriage benchmarks.

There can be some variation in the order of these steps depending on your age, religion, sexual orientation, and the general expectations of your family and social network, but not much. Breakups of all kinds then are seen as a failure because you did not get to the top of the escalator, you didn't "complete" the relationship and making it all the way to the top is seen as the entire purpose of romantic relationships. As we saw in the chapter on commitment and faithfulness, relationship anarchists and other non-monogamous people pioneered taking apart the relationship escalator and picking and choosing what, exactly, you would like out of each relationship and in what order. Polyamorous people have also worked to reframe the conclusion of a romantic relationship, what we would call a "breakup," away from being an inherent failure and toward being an intentional and sometimes even *good* decision. We've also introduced new options that the relationship escalator and the binary breakup framework don't allow for, in particular: relationship de-escalation. In the relationship escalator framework, relationships can only move in one direction. Once you move in together, you are expected to always live together unless the relationship ends. It is the same, especially, for marriage. But it doesn't have to be that way. De-escalation offers an option to move out from living with a romantic partner but still stay romantically intertwined. You could end your romantic relationship and transition to a platonic friendship. *Multiamory* podcast host Emily not only transitioned her relationship with co-hosts Dedecker and Jase from romantic partner to friend, she *maintained* and even *strengthened* their relationship as business partners.

A type of relationship escalator is often present in religious communities, too. Once you see it, you may start noticing it everywhere. I hope here that some polyamorous wisdom can improve the health of your community. In many faith communities, there is a path from casual visitor to regular attendee to volunteer to lay leader and even sometimes to board member. Eager spiritual seekers get swept up in this type of new relationship and are often eager to contribute. Unfortunately, once someone *starts* volunteering, it is often hard for them to *stop* volunteering or to pull back their commitments without making an abrupt break. If you are a leader in a faith community, how might you change your culture so that volunteer leaders are able to pull back their obligations without shame, regret, or excuse? How might you promote de-escalation as a viable option so that members can continue to be active, engaged participants in the life of your community with fewer, or different, responsibilities? If you are a volunteer leader yourself and you find that you want to step back while staying connected, this is your sign that you are allowed to do just that.

There are, however, limits to the high-minded ideal of de-escalation. Some relationships *need* to end, and permanently. This is definitely the case in a relationship where abuse or even deeply entrenched harmful conflict is present. It would be irresponsible and even unsafe to try to simply de-escalate in these contexts. A clean break and even having no contact is a valid choice, too. It also may be the case that moving too quickly from serious romantic partners to friends or business partners may be harmful to one or more of the people involved. If one person wants the romantic relationship to continue while the other doesn't, or if one or both partners are still harboring a lot of hurt feelings, de-escalating may be too painful.

I wish we had better rituals for when relationships ended—

whether a total breakup or some sort of de-escalation. Here, I think our relationships could learn from some spiritual wisdom. The Jewish grieving practice of *shiva* and the Jewish divorce process of a *get* are two rituals whose wisdom could be brought into the sphere of relationships.

When my best friend Josh was dying, everyone knew what to do. I, and Josh's three other closest friends, gathered at the apartment he shared with his partner Sam to take care of their dog and ferry any needed supplies up to Sam at the hospital, as Sam spent the final hours or days by Josh's side. Dan, one of my partner's former partners—and now his very good friend—called my partner to say: "I'm bringing coffee and bagels for everyone. Text me your order. I'll be there in 30." He showed up with the coffee and bagels and then just sat there with us. After Josh died, Brandon sent soup, John sent a DoorDash gift card, a co-worker dropped off groceries. The four of us picked up Sam from the hospital and shared a taxi home together. We had a big grown-up sleepover that night. Only some of our friends are Jewish, but we've all lived in New York City long enough to have adopted many of the best practices of Jewish mourning. While there wasn't an official *shiva* for Josh, who was not Jewish, Dan's simple bagel run and his quiet presence reminded me of many of the *shiva* visits I've made in my life.

A year or so before Josh died, I went through my first major polyamorous breakup. My partner of nearly three years and I decided to end our romantic relationship. We told my other partner Peter, and most of our friends, and then we went on with life the next day, almost as if nothing had happened. No one called to check up on me, no one took me out to dinner, no one dropped off groceries. In his and my efforts to be "mature" and "responsible" and focus on "de-escalating" our relationship, we tried to glide seamlessly from lover to friend, with no formal ritual to transition our status. The following year was rough on both of us as we both tried to navigate our new friendship and lingering, complicated feelings for one another. I spent a lot of time crying: crying while Peter, whom I was living with, was out on a run; crying quietly in the shower; crying before bed and crying again in the morning. Six months into our "de-escalation," where we were friends but also still said "I love you" and spent significant amounts of time together, we had an emotional walk-and-talk where I proposed restarting our romantic relationship. He was not interested. It was utterly devastating. It was a bizarre experience to have my romantic relationship end shortly before Josh's death and then have the final chapter close on that relationship a few months after Josh's death. Breaking up and dying are, obviously, not on the same level at all. My former partner is still very much alive and thriving. I even talk with him every now and then. I would take a breakup over a death any day. But the experience *in my body* of the two was eerily similar.

I'm not the only one to notice this. Jason Silva, a pop philosopher who muses on topics such as life, death, meaning, purpose, romance, and art to over 500,000 subscribers on his "Shots of Awe" YouTube channel, talks about how one of the purposes that romance serves is to stave off the existential dread of mortality. Through romantic relationships, we build whole inner worlds where time stands still and where we and our partner are perfect, almost god-like in our radiance (at least for each other). And so when relationships end, we are confronted with "existential impotence." How is it possible that this thing that was real and true is now gone? In our love for each other, we had built a whole future for ourselves and now it is gone. When this partner and I were still together, I would often imagine the dog we would one day have together, the cabin in the woods he wanted to build together, what his hand would feel like at 40 or 50 or 80 as I held it in mine. And now, all those imaginations, that seemed so *real* at the time, are gone. "Breakups are death practice," Silva notes in the opening title card to one his videos. The tightness in my chest, the waves of tears, the future that never would be, I experienced them in many of the same ways as when people I love have died. I wrote in my journal, "Breaking up is ripping out each stitch in the fabric of your future, one thread at a time." It is the process of erasing the story you had previously written for your future and starting to write a new one over top of it.

This is a moment where spiritual traditions have a wealth of wisdom to offer all of us—and especially non-monogamous people—as we end or transition away from meaningful relationships.

When a Jewish person dies, there is a robust, regimented process that kicks off from the moment of death that extends for 11 months. At the moment a close family member (child, parent, sibling, spouse) learns of the death of their family member, they become an *onen*, which means "someone in between," and virtually all obligations—social and religious—are suspended until after the seven-day mourning period called *shiva*. They tear their clothes (or, in many communities, a small piece of fabric that is then pinned to their clothes). This is a physical manifestation of grief and the tearing apart of the relationship. After burial, *shiva* begins for seven days. During that time, the mourning family members remain together at their home and are visited by extended family, friends, and community who bring food, take care of chores, and are physically present to witness the grief. After *shiva*, mourners enter the 30-day period of *shloshim* where they begin taking on some—but not all—of their former obligations. Then after 30 days, life begins to slowly transition back to normalcy. For the 11 months after death, immediate family members will say *Kaddish*, a prayer of mourning, daily. The Jewish mourning process begins with time standing still at the moment of death—or the moment of hearing of death—and then gradually ushers the mourners slowly back to life, first at burial, then after seven days, then after 30 days, then after 11 months.

I wish that on the day that relationship ended, I was able to fully understand the enormity of what was ending—and I wish my friends and family around me could see it too. I wish I had had more support over the weeks, months, and year that followed. I know I am not alone. Many of the polyamorous people I work with talk of the cold indifference they are met with during breakups, from monogamous friends and family who write off their pain and imagine their relationships "don't count." Imagine, whatever your relationship configuration is, what it would feel like to be carried and supported by your community for an entire year after the end of a major relationship. Make this a new paragraph and change to:

There is one more religious ritual we can look to that w help guide and support our relationship transitions. In a Jewish wedding, partners agree on and sign a *ketubah*, a written wedding contract that details the specific commitments each partner makes to the other, as well as how partners will provide for one another in the event of divorce. Historically, the *ketubah* made explicit the man's obligations to his wife. Developed in a time when men could divorce their wife for any reason, leaving her vulnerable and often destitute, the *ketubah* put protections in place to see that she would be taken care of. In the spirit of egalitarianism, many modern Jewish couples—both straight and queer—use their *ketubah* to make mutual commitments to one another. Just as a Jewish marriage begins with both ritual and paperwork, so too do they end in ritual and paperwork. Historically (and still in Orthodox and many Conservative communities), when a Jewish couple wished to divorce, not only did they need to get a civil divorce, the husband would have a *get* (a Jewish divorce contract) written up and would present it, in the presence of two witnesses, to his wife. If she wished to accept it, she would take it into her hands, raise it up, tuck it under her arm, and then walk a few steps. At that point, the marriage was officially over.

A type of relationship ending or transitioning ritual can be powerful for people of all relationship structures. In the year after polyamory expert and author Jessica Fern and her ex-husband David Cooley got divorced, they decided to do an "un-vowing" where they formally and ritually released their wedding vows, followed by a re-vowing, where they made new commitments to each other as co-parents and what they called "attachment humans"—someone you can count on to help you meet your physical, emotional, and spiritual needs.

The Talmud teaches that whenever someone gets divorced, the very altar of God cries. I'm pretty pro-divorce. Or at least divorce neutral. My own wedding vows intentionally did not promise "until death do you part" but rather "for as long as I am able." There are some times when the relationship *needs* to end and the feelings that accompany a relationship dissolution are varied from grief to joy to relief to confusion and sometimes all of the above! Still, in most cases, no matter how the relationship progressed, evolved, or deteriorated, that line from the Talmud is a recognition that something that was once very meaningful is now gone. Whether you are fully breaking up or de-escalating, whether you were married or not, there can be power in marking the end of the relationship with just as much intentionality and solemnity as you began it. Whether the relationship ending was wanted or unwanted, there is almost always a period of grief, a readjustment of your sense of self, a reorienting of yourself in the world. While you may not need a year long, daily ritual like the *Mourner's Kaddish* and your now-ex partner may or may not want to participate in a secular, polyamorous version of a *get*, I encourage you to find or make some rituals that are meaningful to you.

When one of my non-monogamous relationship coaching clients went to drop off the paperwork that would make his divorce final, he wore the same baseball hat he'd worn on their first date and had a bite to eat at the cafe they had frequented together. After he left the courthouse, he took off the hat and treated himself to a solo date night at a restaurant he'd grown to love since their separation. I've worked with clients who have gone on one final date, written letters they sent and letters they burned, given away or sold or destroyed their ex's belongings, smashed plates in their backyard, and taken themselves on a honeymoon-esque vacation. If someone you love is going through a breakup, especially if they are non-monogamous or their relationship was otherwise not taken seriously, you can do a real blessing by seeing and supporting them in the complexity of their grief.

Sometimes, relationships need to end. When a friend or client tells me their romantic relationship has ended, I have a practice of asking, "How do you feel about that?" rather than jumping to, "I'm sorry." Sometimes a relationship ending is a victory or a relief. Sometimes it's a shock or a heartache. Sometimes it's all of those and more. As relationships end, having clear boundaries is as important as ever. It can also be as difficult as ever. Polyamorous people sometimes feel pressure to "de-escalate" their relationships rather than "break up" with clean and total separation. If the wisdom of polyamory is that love and relationships can look all sorts of ways, then why do we have to follow the script that once our romantic relationship ends, we have to completely cut the person out of our life? That's a fair question to ask! Let's not take anything for granted. It's true, many people are able to successfully de-escalate their romantic relationship into a friendship or a casual friends-with-benefits situation. This is another area where polyamorous people of all orientations find overlap with LGBTQ+ people of all relationship structures: many of our friends are also our exes. Sometimes though, a clean break is needed, either temporarily or permanently; and always, clear boundaries are needed in order to keep everyone safe, sane, and healthy.

Breaking up with God

This framework can also be applied to our faith lives. Sometimes our relationship with religion is so fraught, so hurtful, that we need a clean break. In my work with LGBTQ+ people of faith, most of whom come from conservative Christian backgrounds (though I have also worked with former Orthodox Jews and conservative Muslims, as well), I see first-hand the desire to continue being a "good Christian," a "good Muslim," a "traditionally observant Jew." You might want to keep or transition your relationship with your faith of origin rather than abandon it completely. Let me first say, I fully support this. In fact, my work is built around making sure all people of faith are able to find safe spiritual homes. In my relationship coaching practice, I see time and again that the couples who are able to maintain the closest, or at least the most healthy, friendships after their breakup are the ones who have the clearest boundaries and the cleanest breaks at first. Only after the old patterns—which led to the need for the relationship breakup/transition in the first place—are broken, can new healthy ones be established.

One of my friends continued living with his ex-boyfriend for months after their breakup. Not only did they live together, they shared a bed. During this period, he insisted that they remained friends and on good terms but it was clear to everyone that this arrangement was straining them both. It also, understandably, was a hurdle to them pursuing other relationships or even having the much-needed alone time to process the breakup and heal. By the time they moved out, their post-relationship-friendship was ruptured beyond repair. I can contrast that experience to friends and clients who, when deciding to break up or de-escalate their relationship, have taken a period of time to establish separate identities, routines, and patterns. They have given themselves space to process, grieve, and heal, and to return with a fresh perspective on how and if they would like to relate in the future. Some of these former couples became good friends, while others ultimately went their separate ways and are no longer in regular communication. Sometimes, the most loving thing you can do is let someone go. Sometimes you can be committed to keeping the door open, but do so from a distance that feels safe and comfortable for you. This is true for your romantic relationships as well as your relationship with the divine.

In her book *Polywise*, Jessica Fern[52] teaches a model for handling shifting paradigms and other types of tricky relationship transitions that she calls "temporary vessels." In the framework of non-monogamy, vessels a partnership might try include:

- a staggered approach to dating others
- an experimental period of non-monogamy
- a phase of exclusivity
- temporary poly fidelity (a closed polyamorous relationship, where all partners in the relationship are not engaged in sexual or romantic connection with anyone outside the relationship)
- taking a pause.

Fern explains that one purpose of a temporary vessel is to give "your beleaguered nervous system a much-needed breather," to "slow down your relational explorations," and to "get your feet back under you." If you have a fraught relationship with God or with a particular spiritual community, you might benefit from a spiritual temporary vessel while you sort what comes next for you and if (or how) you will continue to relate to God or if a breakup is necessary. One of the benefits of a temporary vessel is that it takes the pressure off of having to make "the right" decision. It is intentionally temporary. You aren't making any permanent decisions, you're testing out some experiments. Pick a period of time for your temporary vessel and decide it in advance. You can, of course, change your mind along the way but having a finish line in sight will give your brain and your heart some relief. I recommend at least six weeks and ideally no more than six months, a year at most. If your temporary vessel timeline is too long, it will feel more permanent than temporary. Here are some temporary vessels you might try:

- Take a break from attending services at your current spiritual community.
- Temporarily step down from leadership positions.
- Take a break from attending religious services *anywhere*.
- Read books from spiritual thinkers outside your faith tradition or from other parts of your faith tradition or from different types of people within your faith tradition that you are used to.
- Go spiritual speed dating: make a list of congregations in your area and visit each one a few times.
- Stop reading your Bible.
- Focus on *learning about* your faith rather than *practicing* it. Read books *about* your faith tradition.
- Spend time in non-religious organizations that align with your values.

When couples break up and are able to spend some significant time apart from one another, they can make clearer decisions about the future of their relationship. When you refuse to break up with a partner who is clearly hurting you, you lose any hope for repairing or rescuing the relationship—or even a friendship. When long-term partners who have hurt one another break up and don't take time apart to heal, they bring all of the old patterns into their new friendship and often sabotage it in the process. You can't heal when you are still deep in the hurt. What I see with recent exes who spend two or more months apart is that when they do reconnect, they have greater clarity about what they want out of their relationship with each other. Some are able to become dear friends, others transition into friendly, but casual, acquaintances, while others decide they are ready to go their separate ways (and some, of course, decide to restart their romantic relationships). The same will be true for you and your relationship with the divine: you may need some time apart to discern the next right, healthy step for you. Do not think of this time apart as abandoning or being abandoned by God. Taking a break with God is often the best thing you can do for your long-term spiritual health. At the end of your break, you will know if you want to re-engage. And if you know you don't want or need to (or can't!), then take the time to grieve. The loss of a way of relating to God, and especially the loss of a particular faith community, is a big loss. Lean on the spiritual wisdom of grief and the polyamorous wisdom of loss to help you get through it.

CHAPTER 11

Hospitality and Care for the Stranger

The act of welcoming a stranger into your midst is considered an act of sacred hospitality in all the major world religions. Buddhism, Hinduism, Judaism, Christianity, and Islam all understand hospitality to be not just a good deed, but an obligation. For all the talk among the world's religions about the importance of care for the stranger, we don't seem to live up to our ideals. Immigration continues to be a hot-button issue across the Americas, Europe, and Asia. Isolationist propaganda was at the heart of Trump's successful 2016 presidential campaign, as well as the United Kingdom's "Brexit" from the European Union. Sacred scripture is full of stories of how immigrants, outsiders, and other strangers should be treated. One of those stories is famous for the wrong reason. The stories of Sodom and Gomorrah have long been (wrongly) associated with the condemnation of LGBTQ+ people. The anti-gay slur "sodomite" comes from this story. But the Bible itself tells a different story and the lesson becomes even more powerful when paired with a polyamorous perspective. If you aren't familiar with the story, here's a quick summary. Then, we'll look at what polyamory can teach us about hospitality and care for the stranger, as well as some new ways that non-monogamous folks can feel blessed in their pursuits.

The Biblical text tells us that two men arrive at the gates of Sodom, a city probably located somewhere near the Dead Sea, as night is falling. Our main character in this story, Lot, sees them and invites them to stay at his place for the evening. They plan to stay in the city square but Lot insists they come home with him. Not long after, a large mob of the city's residents begins to form outside Lot's house. Here, some context is needed. The Talmud offers insight into one understanding of what life in Sodom was like. Jews have an obligation to take care of outsiders, the poor, travelers, and others in need. However, moral corruption was widespread and *Talmud Sanhedrin 109a* describes a corrupt system that the city used to exploit the poor and others in need. Residents would write their name on a coin and then give it to the person in need, thus *technically* fulfilling their obligation. Then, everyone in the town would simply refuse to sell this person any bread. When he eventually died of hunger, all the people who had "given" money to the person in need would come and take back the coins with their names written on them. This same passage of Talmud shares that the people of Sodom said, "Why do we need travelers, as they come only to divest us of our property? Come, let us cause the proper treatment of travelers to be forgotten from our land."

It is against this backdrop of hostility and violence toward the poor and outsiders that the two men enter the city. The mob is enraged that Lot has offered some travelers hospitality. The men of Sodom come seeking to brutalize the visitors, including through sexual violence. Elsewhere in the Bible, the prophet Ezekiel names the sin of Sodom explicitly:[53] "Only this was the sin of your sister Sodom: arrogance! She and her daughters had plenty of bread and untroubled tranquility; yet she did not support the poor and the needy" (16:49). We see the sin of Sodom continue to repeat itself over and over again throughout history. Even I feel indicted by it. Not because I am a queer man, but because of the way the country and cities I am part of treat "the poor and needy." In New York City, where I live, 50 percent of working-age households are struggling to afford basic fixed expenses, according to City Harvest.[54] That is three million people. Beyond that, 1.4 million people are struggling to feed themselves. That's in New York City alone. In the United States in 2023, approximately 650,000 people were living in shelters or on the streets in any given night—which is to say nothing of people forced to stay with family, couch surf between friends' places, squat, or otherwise live in unstable housing. We are a modern-day Sodom.

As we explore the topic of hospitality and care for the stranger, I want to caution against focusing our attention in only one direction: from "us" to the "stranger," as if relationship is always inherently imbalanced and we do the caring. Instead, I would propose that we can be transformed by the stranger too, that in welcoming in others who are not like us, our communities, our relationships, and our faith are enriched by their perspectives and experiences. It is not enough for straight people to welcome LGBTQ+ people, for monogamous people to welcome polyamorous people, or for citizens to welcome immigrants; we must recognize that we are in need of their blessing too. Straight people must learn from the LGBTQ+ people in their midst; monogamous people must learn from the non-monogamous people in their midst. Polyamorous rabbi Nikki DeBlosi's thesis was on this precise topic. "We are told [especially in the United States that] we are supposed to belong to a group that does not just include our own ethnic, spiritual, sexual community. The people who are different from us are also our neighbors."[55] That leads to one of the central questions of her work: "Can you love the stranger and let them be strange?" Can we love, support, accept, and even integrate those who are different from us without requiring them to change to become more like us?

Queer, polyamorous, and sexually liberated people are often pushed to the edges of mainstream culture. Our lives are treated as taboo topics and we often experience a sort of estrangement from our families and faith communities. In that way, we have the experience of being the stranger. But we have also, perhaps because of our experiences on the margins, developed beautiful cultures of care for the strangers in our midst. You can learn a thing or two about being welcoming from those who have been made to feel unwelcome. In the following sections, you'll see examples of hospitality in action and how, in particular, you can learn from those who have historically been pushed to the margins of society on how to welcome well. I hope that the examples and practices will be more than an intellectual exercise and that they will inspire you to reimagine hospitality and being welcoming in your own life, relationship, family, and communities and that you will proactively try out new ways of being welcoming so that you, too, can be transformed in the process.

HIV/AIDS is a polyamorous issue

When the AIDS epidemic broke out in the 1980s, the government and wider culture was quick to define it as someone else's problem: gay men, drug users, immigrants, and Black Americans. These were people who had been forced to the margins, made into an "other," and then blamed for their own perceived failures. The specter of AIDS specifically and sexually transmitted infections more generally was used to condemn sexual liberation, which gay men were on the front lines of. A 1978 study[56] looking at the diverse experiences of gay men and women found significant levels of non-monogamy among gay male respondents. While the study did not look at "monogamy," "open relationships," and "polyamory" in the ways we understand them today, even among gay male "close couples" (defined by having marriage-like arrangements with a partner and fewer incidents of cruising and lower number of sexual partners) diverse sexual exploration was common. For many of these men, a "close couple" did not necessarily mean a "closed couple."

In the 2010s I worked as the senior director of marketing and communications at Harlem United, a health center and community advocacy organization that advanced health equity through health-care, housing, and harm reduction. It began in the late 1980s as an "agency of last resort." Community activists, faith leaders, and a few justice-minded health professionals had noticed that too many peo-ple—particularly low-income or homeless Black men and women living with HIV/AIDS in upper Manhattan—were being neglected outright by existing services. This was especially true for people whose mental health or drug use contributed to additional obstacles for accessing and staying in care. An overloaded and underfunded healthcare system exacerbated these problems. Our chief medical officer spoke often of her experiences working at Harlem Hospital, where patients far outnumbered rooms and gravely ill men with AIDS were left on cots in the hallways. It was an overwhelming scene requiring an overwhelming response. When we talk about the re-sponse to the HIV/AIDS crisis, we remember the queerness of the countless individuals who contributed to the cause, and we recognize that organizations such as ACT UP, Gay Men's Health Crisis, and Treatment Action Group were let by LGBTQ+ people. I would also like us to remember and celebrate the ways in which non-monog-amous values were also at the heart of much of this liberating and life-saving work. Polyamory has always been a part of public health; we just need to remember to look for it.

When we talk about "polyamory issues," a number of topics are of-ten front of discussion: non-discrimination protections, family plan-ning, greater social acceptance, and dating difficulties, in addition to widely applicable topics that are particularly relevant to polyamorous people (and which we have particular insight into), such as com-munication, jealousy, and breaking up. For instance, the Southwest

Love Fest, a premier non-monogamy focused conference, has workshops on jealousy, grief, neurodivergence, spirituality, joy, mental health, and more. While sexual health is often a part of discussions of non-monogamy, it is often in the context of personal practices to reduce your risk of acquiring or transmitting a sexually transmitted infection. There is an opportunity for all of us—monogamous and non-monogamous—to broaden our conversation around sexual health in relationships from the individual to the societal. ACT UP recognized that "Don't have sex" or "Just use condoms" was insufficient to address the public health crisis that HIV/AIDS posed. It is important for polyamorous communities to remember that while destigmatizing conversations about personal sexual health and providing robust tools for safer sex and harm reduction practices are important, our commitments as non-monogamous people cannot stop at our own bedroom doors. There is a coalition-building opportunity here for us to translate our own sexual expertise into public policy priorities that will benefit people of all relationship structures.

Candy Marcum was a lesbian and a therapist working with a small private practice in Texas when she met Howie Daire, a fellow queer mental health provider, and together they started an LGBTQ+ counseling center in 1982. At the time, Daire, through his friendships and connections in bigger cities like New York and San Francisco, saw how HIV/AIDS, then called GRID ("gay-related immunodeficiency"), was spreading among the gay communities there. "He could see it, certainly better than I could," according to Marcum, and so they started a GRID support hotline at their practice. Unfortunately, Daire started getting sick not long after they began their practice. While Marcum was already seeing multiple HIV+ men free of charge, she partnered with Daire's mother to take care of him as he grew more and more sick, eventually losing his vision to cytomegalovirus and dying at home in the summer of 1986. Candy Marcum continued to take care of gay men dying of AIDS through free therapy, as well as more community-based care such as home and hospital visits. "My clients were getting sick, my friends were getting sick...My colleagues, the people that I [shared the] office with and did psychotherapy with, were dying."[57] She talked with them and helped them get their affairs in order and, when the time came, at their request, she spoke at many of their funerals. "It was never, never an easy thing." But she kept doing it. Over and over and over she "gird[ed] up her loins" and went and did it. To this day, she's still taking care of gay men in Texas. Candy Marcum is one of countless lesbian women who took care of gay men dying of AIDS.

In the Gospel of Mathew, Jesus tells a parable in which some people are set to inherit the Kingdom of God because "I was hungry and you gave me something to eat, I was thirsty and you gave me something to drink, I was a stranger and you invited me in, I needed clothes and you clothed me, I was sick and you looked after me, I was in prison and you came to visit me." Confused, these people ask, basically, "When did we do this?" and God replies, "Whatever you did for one of the least of these brothers and sisters of mine, you did for me." In Judaism, visiting and taking care of the sick is not just a value, but a *mitzvah*, a sacred obligation called *bikur cholim*. A generation of LGBTQ+ people—many, maybe even most, of whom were non-monogamous—are modern saints, embodying the highest ideals of hospitality and care for the stranger. May their memories be a blessing and may our lives be an honor to theirs.

Slutty hospitality

Literal sluttiness isn't the *only* way to practice hospitality in one area so that you might find ways to apply it more broadly in others. To go back to Leviticus 19, the passages instruct Israelites to "love [the stranger] as yourself, for you were strangers in the land of Egypt."

There is a clear connection to the Israelites' experience as outsiders and their ethical responsibility and ability to care for the strangers in their midst. In what ways have *you* been put on the outside? How can you draw on these experiences to see to it that others who cross your path feel included instead? How can you find small ways to practice hospitality, so that slowly and surely you can build up those welcoming skills to create a more inclusive world?

Given how much overlap there is between LGBTQ+ and polyamorous communities, and the ways in which religion has been used as a cudgel against us, I imagine most readers are familiar with a certain passage in Leviticus: "You shall not lie with a man as with a woman, for it is an abomination." But do you know, Leviticus is one of my favorite books of the Bible? Just one chapter later, we get this gem:

> When an immigrant sojourns with you in your land, you shall not do him wrong. You shall treat the stranger who sojourns with you as the native among you, and you shall love him as yourself, for you were strangers in the land of Egypt: I am the Lord your God.

It is one of many verses in the book, and in the Bible more generally, emphasizing our responsibility to take care of each other and *especially* to take care of strangers and immigrants. Being in a foreign country is a vulnerable experience. You may not know the language, you may have limited connections, you have to rely on the kindness of others. Many forms of non-monogamy are daily practices in hospitality. How can I make my metamour—my partner's partner—more comfortable? How can my partners and I share household responsibilities? How can we welcome guests into our own home? Two of the three main models for polyamory, "kitchen table polyamory" and "garden party polyamory," imply a level of welcome, openness, and hospitality to them. Kitchen table polyamory is a way of relating where everyone connected romantically—one's partners and their partners—feels comfortable sitting down to a big group meal together. In kitchen table polyamory, metamours and other members of a polycule would usually consider themselves friends and have some level of engagement in each other's lives. In garden party polyamory, partners and metamours are not close friends, nor do they have interdependent lives, but they would be comfortable spending time together in a large, casual group setting such as a garden party. These traditional images of polyamorous hospitality are also very family- and romance-centric. I'd like to propose that it's not only "love" and "relationships" in polyamory that can serve as models for us. We can learn hospitality from promiscuous and even anonymous one-night-stand versions of non-monogamy.

A few years ago, I went over to the apartment of a guy I'd hooked up with a few times before. We had a strictly casual relationship. He knew I was in an open relationship; I knew he was only in the country for a year for grad school. We were friendly, but we only ever met for sex. This particular day, I popped out of my home office for a mid-day fling. He met me at the door to his apartment and silently escorted me to his bedroom and we began to have sex. As we started, I felt something just wasn't right. The physical logistics weren't lining up quite right and we had to take a pause. And in that pause, I realized there was something more going on. I leaned forward and kissed him, and pulled him sideways so that we flopped down on the bed next to each other, naked and intertwined.

"What's wrong?" I asked.

"I can't start talking about it or I won't stop crying," he replied.

So we sat in silence for a few moments and then he began to tell me about the boy who was breaking his heart. And then, like he said he would, he started crying. I held him and kissed his cheek gently and ran my fingers through his hair as he choked back the tears and continued to tell the story.

We lay there, our bodies laid bare as physical offerings to each other as he poured out his heart and I received it. I ran my fingers softly through his curly brown hair and dabbed a small tear out of the corner of his eye with my thumb. I watched as his head bobbed up and down, rising and falling with each one of my breaths and with my right hand wrapped around his waist, I felt the in and out of his breath, noticed as it slowly but surely calmed from harsh and erratic to slow and smooth. When he had let the weight go from his chest and the tears dried from his eyes, we lay there some more as the afternoon sun streaked across our chests and warmed our skin. Then it was time to go; him to a grad-school class, me back to my home office. I pulled up my jeans as he pulled on his sweatpants, and we walked down the rusty New York City stairs and out into the warm autumn afternoon and kissed goodbye one last time before parting ways. To see another person in the fullness of who they are and the complexity of what they desire, to hold their vulnerable naked body, is hospitality too.

I have invited more strangers into my house than I can count. I don't know if that makes me a saint; I think it mostly makes me a slut. Perhaps it makes me a little of both. It takes incredible courage to welcome a complete stranger into your home from a dating or hookup app, or to bring someone home from a club or a party, to be in a physically compromising position, sometimes even to fall asleep next to this person whose name you don't know. Every one-night stand is a rejection of a dogma that says strangers are scary, that you must guard your heart and your home tightly. Every time you open your heart, or your door, or your legs, you say, "I choose welcome."

There is a dance that happens in anonymous or one-night-only sexual encounters. If it's going to be any good at all, you have to skillfully manage a number of elements of the encounter. You have to quickly establish chemistry. You have to be willing to be clear with what you want through either verbal or non-verbal communication.

As you peel off each other's clothes, you are placing trust that this stranger will respect and honor what they see (or, consensually and skillfully disrespect and degrade you in a way that leaves you all hot and bothered). You are placing trust in the other person to receive your desires and fantasies and you are holding a sacred space to receive theirs. There are many ways to be welcoming, and show hospitality and care for the stranger. Christian churches "pass the peace"; in Judaism we give *tzedakah*. In Hinduism, the unexpected guest, called the *atithi*, is to be treated as God.[58] A blowjob can be a blessing too, an orgy a sacred welcome. If the citizens of Sodom had acted more like patrons of a queer bathhouse, they just may have been spared destruction.

Welcoming the stranger takes practice

A promiscuous style of relating is a regular practice of hospitality, vulnerability, trust, and mutual respect and care. To see what this non-monogamous experience can teach us all about practicing expansive hospitality, we need to take a detour through Buddhist meditation. Pema Chodron explains[59] the purpose of meditation in Buddhism:

> Sitting meditation, also known as mindfulness-awareness practice, is the foundation of bodhicitta training. [Bodhicitta is the wish to attain enlightenment and to bring all beings to the same awakened state.]
>
> Sitting meditation gives us a way to move closer to our thoughts and emotions and to get in touch with our bodies. It is a method of cultivating unconditional friendliness toward ourselves and for parting the curtain of indifference that distances us from the suffering of others. It is our vehicle for learning to be a truly loving person.

A meditation practice happens silently, mostly in your head, and often all by yourself. Even if you practice together with a group, each person is in their own practice. It is no accident that meditation practice is called a "practice." Each time you sit for meditation, you are practicing. You practice paying attention to your body or to your thoughts. You practice noticing your desires and your instincts. You practice being present to calm. You also practice being present to anger, fear, frustration, or any other emotion that may arise. When you practice meditation day in and day out, you train your mind to a new way of working and responding. The practice reverberates throughout your life. When you spend time daily noticing your thoughts, you will be more able to catch them as they begin to run away from you (it is a common meditation technique to silently say to yourself "thinking" when you notice your thoughts running away). When you spend five, ten, or twenty minutes paying attention to your breath each day, you will more quickly notice when your breath starts to quicken when you are scared or angry. When you practice choosing not to scratch your itching ear during a seated meditation, you practice acting with intention rather than impulse. Perhaps then it will be easier to wait a few moments before responding to the stressful email from a co-worker, rather than lashing out in anger.

In meditation, we practice neutrality and non-reactivity in our mind so that when we get up from the cushion and get out into our life, we might apply that same neutrality and non-reactivity in action. In the same way, when you practice inviting strangers into your house at night for a hookup, it can become easier to see the stranger on the street as friendly rather than dangerous. When you let them into your bedroom with your watch and wallet on the table, it may be easier to treat hotel staff or cleaning services with trust rather than suspicion. When you practice talking to strangers in clubs or bars or backrooms or apps, it might be easier to talk to your neighbor. Of course, it may be that low-commitment sex doesn't interest you, isn't readily available, or is unsafe for you,* or you may be in a monogamous relationship where such encounters would be a breach of your relationship agreements.

Slutty hospitality for the monogamous-minded

Monogamous relationships can take on a Sodom-like quality—quick to isolate outsiders and to protect the core couple at all costs—if you aren't careful. The "Castle Doctrine" is a legal doctrine which exists to varying degrees in all U.S. states and in many countries around the world and defines a person's home as their metaphoric "castle." It gives them a presumption of the right to use force—including lethal force—to defend themselves in it. While there is good legal reason for this doctrine, the mindset of "my family and I are a castle unto ourselves" can lead to isolationist practices. Most Americans live in private homes with their immediate family (whether that's an apartment, condo, house). Three-quarters of Americans drive alone to work. Once at work, most of us interact with the same set of co-workers day in and day out, if we interact with them at all. Some of us spend the overwhelming majority of our day alone in offices or cubicles, while others are alone on assembly lines or factory floors. Service workers have brief and shallow interactions with customers, but since they are working, must also perform additional emotional labor in these conversations to seem happy and agreeable, regardless of what the customer throws at them. Only half of Americans[60] are

---

*This could be for any number of reasons. You are an LGBTQ+ person who does not live near many other LGBTQ+ people, you have a physical disability that requires planning for accommodation in order to have sex, or because of your age, skin color, body type, HIV status, gender identity, or any number of other reasons, you find it difficult to have casual sex regularly—or to do so in a way that feels safe to you.

"very satisfied" or "completely satisfied" with the number and quality of their friendships.

We'll get into the importance of not just friendship, but also community, in the following chapter. But for now, I want to focus on what this means for hospitality and care for others. Most of us are ill-practiced at meeting new people. For the first 18-years of my life, I lived in the suburbs. Then I went to college in one of the most notoriously car-centric major cities: Los Angeles. The only new people I happened to meet were people who lived in the same suburb, went to the same school, or worked at the same place as me. Sure, I occasionally went to coffee shops or restaurants or bookstores but they were largely inaccessible without a car and inconvenient to anyone who did not live nearby. I would sometimes see people asking for money on the street corner, but always through a car window. It was not until I moved to New York City at the age of 22 that I had my first conversation with a homeless person. In 2019, the New York City subway moved 5.5 million people every single day. At the peak of rush hour, you could be packed into a subway car with up to 200 other people.[61] I probably saw more new people in my first day of commuting to work in New York City than I did in a decade in suburban Maryland. We don't all need to live in cities, certainly not in New York City, but we do need more opportunities to meet new people and interact with strangers. Can you say a quick and casual hello to an unfamiliar co-worker at the office? Can you volunteer once a month with a local charity? Can you check in a little extra on a friend who told you he was going through a tough time? Can you leave your front door unlocked for an evening or an hour or even just a few minutes? If you can offer a stranger an orgasm, perhaps you can offer your neighbor some home-cooked soup when she is sick.

Taking care of each other is not just an individual pursuit. It will take community action and public policy. The fewer connections—and especially casual connections—you have, the more insulated and insular your life becomes. One hundred years ago, the downtown districts of American cities were dotted with small shops, restaurants, offices, apartments, and parks and were filled with pedestrians on foot. A shift in urban planning priorities toward cars now sees those same districts full of multi-lane streets and parking lots, and cut up by highways. As our cities become less walkable, our opportunities for chance encounters go down. That takes a toll on us. "Regular interactions with acquaintances—the local coffee barista, for example—make people happier," writes Zara Abrams[62] for the American Psychological Association. It also makes us less able to take care of the stranger. In neighborhoods with slow, safe streets and a mix of shops and housing, there are more "eyes on the street," as author and urban activist Jane Jacobs called them.[63] The business owner on the corner can keep an eye on your kids playing in the front yard or street while you are at work, and you will notice if someone is meddling with her business over the weekend. This type of neighborhood reimagining will, of course, not directly address issues like income equality, racial discrimination, police violence, or other types of safety. Nor will it provide much-needed support to people experiencing food insecurity or homelessness. But it will give you a more robust perspective on your community, more practice at encountering strangers, and more understanding of the diverse experiences of your community. Taking care of each other is easier the more we know each other. This will make our lives richer, our communities safer, and our society more just.

Your strong friends need care too

While I believe there is much strength, insight, and actionable tactics to be learned from polyamorous and non-monogamous people on how to take care of others well, we need care too. Polyamorous people experience hostility and rejection too. For individuals, families, and communities who are monogamous, I'd like to propose that your faith might call you to welcome the polyamorous people in your midst and to do so in a way that honors our differences, rather than asks us to conform. This will require both personal and systemic change. You will need to question and redefine your ideas of love, commitment, family, and fidelity (I hope inspired by the stories in this book). It should affect how you talk about these topics in both casual conversations and from public pulpits. Your institutions may need to change as well: you may need to redefine the requirements for family memberships at your congregation, for healthcare benefits at your company, or for wedding and commitment ceremonies to be performed by your clergy.

In my work with non-monogamous people over the past six years, I've observed a few common themes for what being welcoming looks like in practice. Many of us want to be able to share our whole selves with the people we care about. If you know a friend or family member has multiple partners, asking about all of them—not just the one they've been with longest, or live with, or are married to—can go a long way. When planning social gatherings and inviting partners of your friends and family, explicitly stating that all partners are welcome will go a long way. Pay extra attention if you are close with both partners in a long-term relationship and one or both of them has partners you don't know as well. Be explicit in your welcome so that no one feels left out! This is especially helpful for gatherings where there is no cost to bring additional guests, but even for more elaborate affairs like weddings or vacations, try to find ways to expand the welcome, such as not assuming which partner your loved one will bring.

While there is still limited formal research on polyamorous lives, relationships, and experiences, a 2021 study by Ryan Witherspoon found that nearly two-thirds of polyamorous people have experienced some form of prejudice or discrimination based on their non-monogamous identity and/or relationship structure.[64] Types of prejudice and discrimination that respondents reported due to being polyamorous included verbal harassment, sexual harassment, discrimination by medical doctors and mental health practitioners, workplace harassment, rape, and loss of child custody. This precariousness is compounded for non-monogamous people with other marginalized identities such as being LGBTQ+, a person of color, disabled, a woman, or an immigrant, for example. Witherspoon's study validates my own experience and that of many of my relationship coaching clients: the negative reactions of others to our non-monogamy makes life harder. Sometimes, the hurdles we face are systemic and significant, such as overt employment discrimination or the inability to legally marry more than one partner, and the subsequent exclusion from protections and benefits attached to marriage. At other times, the exclusion is subtle or even ambiguous. Small slights add up, like sorting out which partners are or are not invited to weddings or social gatherings, prying questions to discern which partner is the longer (and thus "real") one, and the catch in your friend or family member's throat as they attempt to introduce you and your partners to their friends and family. It is difficult to tease apart a purely logistical decision from a thoughtless mistake or an intentional snub.

If you are non-monogamous, I hope that this experience of othering and outsiderness can spur you to work for greater inclusion for all people, in all aspects of society. For monogamous-minded readers, I hope you take some polyamorous inspiration from this chapter on how you can expand and deepen your welcome and care for *all* people, while also thinking specifically about ways to make sure your communities welcome rather than isolate the non-monogamous stranger at your gate. Our faith and our relationships can be structures that support and inspire us to take better care of those in our midst. The work of welcome is both interpersonal and structural. How you treat other people matters, but it does not stop there. Welcome extends to the policies of your workplace, organization, or congregation, too. Welcome asks us to take a stand to advocate for change of policy at local, national, and international levels. Welcome is your company's non-discrimination policy or your state's non-discrimination laws. Welcome is the stories you tell from the pulpit or bimah. Welcome is outlined in your denomination's liturgies and rites. Welcome is being able to access affordable healthcare without having to be monogamously married. Welcome informs our immigration laws. As we explored in the chapter on love, hospitality and welcome are not just theoretical ideals; they must be grounded in action to be meaningful. How you treat the visitor at your congregation, the laws you advocate for (or ignore) that harass or support homeless people in your community, the policies at your workplace, the attitude toward your friends, the way you treat the face in the grid on a dating app: it all matters.

CHAPTER 12

Breaking Down Barriers

On the 15th anniversary of being with my partner Peter, we got legally married. More than that, we threw a giant queer, cabaret and dance party, complete with a "Rituals & Romance" section dedicated to formalizing our commitment, with both queer and Jewish significance. In the days and weeks after our wedding, friends and family would ask me, "How's married life treating you?" and my answer was always the same, "Not any different from before." Peter and I had been together for 15 years, nearly the entirety of our adult lives, before that moment. I didn't feel as if our relationship was different in any significant ontological way. And yet, it must be different, right? There must have been a reason why we chose to bring 200 of our friends and family together, there must have been a reason to get legally married. I mean, there was a rabbi and a chuppah! That doesn't happen by accident. We planned every moment of the day, from the words we used and didn't use to describe it, to what we emphasized and what we didn't include, to who participated and what they did. For us, the day was a celebration of what already is, not a promise of what is to come. We didn't have to promise to love and support for the rest of our lives because we had already been living that promise for 15 years. I think, perhaps, that our relationship is exactly the same as it was before and yet also something brand new. I'm right in my assessment that nothing is ontologically different, but perhaps something is different after all.

In my own religious tradition, Jews are commanded to "remember the Sabbath, to keep it holy." At the start of Shabbat every Friday night, we say a number of blessings to usher it in. There is much debate about what, exactly, these blessings do. Do we say the blessings as a recognition of what already is: the Sabbath is holy, whether we bless it or not; our blessings are merely an affirmation of what already is. Or do we say the blessings to make, to keep, the Sabbath holy, and it is in and through our blessings that Shabbat becomes holy? If we did not usher it in, would those 25 hours be holy nonetheless? It feels like a similar question to the one Peter and I asked ourselves when considering a social and spiritual ceremony after 15 years together: is our relationship already holy or do these sacraments make it so? I have my own answer to that question, but I'll get to that later.

In Judaism, we have blessings for just about everything: blessings to usher in the Sabbath, blessings when meeting a political leader, blessings before going on a trip, blessings when you see a rainbow, and countless more. Abraham Joshua Heschel was one of Judaism's most prominent modern thinkers. Central to his theology was cultivating and responding to a sense of awe and wonder, what he called "radical amazement."

> Our radical amazement responds to the mystery, but does not produce it. You and I have not invented the grandeur of the sky nor endowed [humankind] with the mystery of birth and death. We do not create the ineffable, we encounter it.[65]

Many of the Jewish blessings can be understood through that lens; they are moments of acknowledgment of awe and wonder that we encounter in our lives. When Peter and I moved from Los Angeles to Maryland, we drove across the county and on our journey, stopped at the Grand Canyon. Thanks to science, I know exactly how the Grand Canyon was formed: over the course of millions of years, the slow movement of water gradually wore down the rock. Through the accumulation of infinitesimally small flecks of rock being chipped loose and carried away, we now have this majestic vista. All of that knowledge didn't stop my heart from dropping in my stomach when I walked out to the very tip of Shoshone Point and gazed down 5,000 feet to the valley below. Of course, my heart didn't even *really* "drop" into my stomach; that too is a metaphorical turn of phrase to acknowledge that while something very specific physically happened (my heartbeat became irregular for a few seconds before returning to normal), I *experienced* that sensation as something with a deeper meaning. I didn't just make that meaning up either; hundreds of thousands of years of evolution developed such a response because when you stand on the edge of a cliff, if your body can scream "PAY ATTENTION," you're much more likely to survive. So my heart skipping those beats *does* in fact point to something else. I don't believe the Grand Canyon points toward a creator; I think it points toward the sheer wondrous luck of our planet's natural forces. But I also think that sitting alone with Peter in silence on the edge of that canyon and taking in the grandeur of it all did something to me, too. In my screen-filled day-to-day life, where the latest social media tirade can feel as if it has earth-shattering importance, taking in the actual shattered earth and seeing, literally seeing, my relative smallness was a meaningful reorder. So I said the blessing for seeing natural wonders: "Praise to You, Adonai our God, Sovereign of the universe, Source of creation and its wonders."

In many ways, the practice of saying blessings in Judaism is like gratitude practices found across many spiritual and secular traditions. While many Jews say blessings, there are other ways you can not just notice and appreciate the "good" things in your life, but also tap into awe and wonder around you:

- Christian grace before a meal.
- A "metta" meditation in Buddhism.
- The "gratitude list" in the popular Five-Minute Journal.
- The "Victory Log"* many bullet journalers and other productivity types use.

One of my favorite blessings in Judaism is a rather obscure one, probably not well-known to those who aren't strictly observant Jews: Asher Yatzar, which is said after going to the bathroom:[66]

Praise to you, Adonai, our God, Sovereign of the universe,
who formed the human body with skill
creating the body's many pathways and openings.
It is well known before Your throne of glory
that if one of them be wrongly opened or closed,
it would be impossible to endure and stand before You.
Blessed are You, Adonai, who heals all flesh, working wondrously.

The reason I'm obsessed with this blessing, in particular, is that it is a reminder there is nothing so profane it cannot be sacred—even poop can be holy. Madeline L'Engle offers a similar reflection, from her perspective as a Christian: "There is nothing so secular it cannot be sacred, and that is one of the deepest meanings of the Incarnation," she wrote in *Walking on Water: Reflections on Faith and Art*.[67] My decades as a polyamorous person have taught me something similar

---

*I first came across this concept in *Wake Up* by Matt Frazier (www.nomeatathlete. com/wake-up-info-full), and have since incorporated versions of it into many of the courses and workshops in the QueerTheology.com membership as well as my relationship coaching practice.

when it comes to relationships: there is no type of relationship that cannot also be holy. This applies to monogamous people, too. No matter your relationship style or structure, all of the different types of relationships you've had and will have over your life can be as meaningful as you'd like them to be. Perhaps you could come up with your own blessing to remind you of that.

What if your best friends are just as important as your romantic partners? What if your fuckbuddies and friends-with-benefits have just as much significance as your spouse? What if your one-night stands can be as meaningful as your decades-long relationships? This is true for me. I have learned deep life lessons that shape who I am from my friends. I had the experience of loving someone other than my partner for the first time, with someone who was a kinky playmate. I discovered new parts of myself in a relationship that lasted just a few years. I've had spiritual revelations from one-night stands in backrooms and back alleys. At QueerTheology.com, we have a 13-issue digital magazine collection called *Spit & Spirit*, with each issue focusing on a different topic. For the SEX(BODIES) issue, I wrote a prayer for the first man I ever had sex with. In the days after that first time, I felt shame about the way that it had gone down: that it was someone I didn't know, that I had been drinking, that there wasn't something "romantic" about it like candles or flowers or at least a date first. But with the perspective of time, I came to appreciate that this one-night stand was beautiful in its own way.

Dear God,
Thank you for John. For the safe &
respectful embrace of his arms, for the
warmth of his chest.

Thank you for his insistence on consent
even while we were drunk, on repeating

the question even though it was my idea,

"Are you sure?"

The teachers in some of your churches
taught me that every time a person has sex,
they leave a part of themselves behind.

Like tape being pulled off a sweater.

It gets dirtier and dirtier each time,
and eventually loses its stickiness.

I no longer believe that, that sex and
intimacy can be reduced so simply, but I do
think I left a part of myself with John. Or, at
least he left a part of himself with me.

That's not a bad thing, though.

I'm grateful for vulnerability, for mine and
for his.

I'm grateful for sex education that taught
me how to be safe.

I'm grateful for parents who asked me
to wait until I was absolutely sure I was
ready...and to be absolutely safe when I
was.

I'm grateful for pleasure. For the head

rush and the sweating and the swelling.

The sweet kisses and gentle nibbles and
pulling on hair.

I'm grateful for sighs and heaving chests
and restful sleep.

I'm grateful for time and perspective. I
remember being upset with myself for
"messing up" my first, for someone I wasn't
in a relationship with, for not having
candles or roses or chocolate or something
more "romantic," I guess. I'm grateful that
I've learned to see that first times can be
any number of ways and still be good. I'm
grateful that I still smile when I pass him
on the street or meet him in my dreams.

I'm grateful for John.

When I shared that reflection with our community, I was over-whelmed by the outpouring of messages I received in response. So many people had similar first times and had similarly been made to feel ashamed. In a world that prioritizes long-term, committed, monogamous relationships, anything other than that can feel like a mistake. Polyamory taught me that all different types of relation-ships can be meaningful and once I learned that, I could look back at my past and see it in a whole new light. Years after I wrote that prayer, I moved back to Los Angeles, where he still lived, and as luck would have it, we popped up on each other's dating/hookup app grids. We got together to catch up on our lives over the past decade. We talked about our respective partners. I told him about the prayer and he asked me to read it to him. And then we fucked again, for the first time since that night. And it was good. It was very good.

Blessed are You, Adonai our God, Sovereign of the Universe, Who knows the relationships that will guide us through our life. It is well known and obvious before your throne of glory that if any one of them had started earlier, or gone on longer, or never happened at all, we could not possibly be who we are. We are forever changed by the people who cross our paths. Blessed are you, Adonai, Who delights in the process of our becoming.

"Who is my family?" "Who is my partner?"

"This is Steven, he's my, uh..."

I don't know exactly how to finish that sentence. There are any number of descriptors that are true and accurate. He's my good friend. He's my kinky play partner. He's someone I love dearly. From the outside, if I didn't have a husband, it would probably look as if we are dating. We met on a hookup app. Our hooking up grew into quality time together, outside the bedroom too. We go to dinners, movies, and protests together. We make out on the dance floor at gay clubs. He holds my hand whenever we go for a drink at the bar, and sometimes while just walking down the street. We cuddle on the couch and occasionally have sleepovers. We do all of that and yet we are, explicitly, "not boyfriends." In fact, he told me once, "I love you, but I don't want to be your boyfriend." We exist in a liminal space: more than friends but not boyfriends, partners, or spouses. It is a way of relating without a clear label, yet among my friends and clients, I have encountered more of these types of "relationships" than I can count.

The practice of blurring relational lines can be another entry into deepening your spirituality. As with government policy, the official demarcations of family of many of the world's religions are quite strict. The real story of how we relate is much blurrier, though. While almost no government recognizes marriages of more than two people (and those that do allow it only for men and only under certain conditions), polyamorous relationships continue to thrive even without official sanction. Likewise, there are no mainstream religions or denominations that widely recognize polyamorous relationships, and most still define family as your family of origin, and yet polyamorous people continue to be integral parts of diverse faith communities. While traditional religious law and culture draw family lines around blood and marriage, there have always been undercurrents in spiritual traditions that recognize and emphasize a blurring of boundaries. Polyamory reminds us to remember these radical roots.

In most Christian churches, memberships are offered to individuals and families (spouses and children). You'll find family-themed services for parents and their children. Many have small groups for singles, married young adults, and parents with families. Over and over again, the nuclear family is prioritized. This is true even among progressive churches, many of which emphasized married, monogamous couples in their support for LBGTQ+ marriage equality. It's even more true in conservative churches who see the relationship between God and man (literally, men) to be a parallel to the relationships of husband and wife, and parents and children. The family you are born to is of primary importance. And yet, the Gospels of Matthew, Mark, and Luke each contain a curious scene of Jesus complicating the centrality of nuclear family. In each version of the story, Jesus's mother and brothers come to visit him. The crowd Jesus is speaking with tells him they are here to see him and Jesus responds by blurring who exactly family is. In Mark and Matthew, he asks, "Who is my mother, and who are my brothers?" In all three accounts, he goes on to state that his mother and siblings are the people who are gathered there with him, the people who share in his mission. To a modern, non-Jewish reader of these stories, Jesus's question "Who is my mother? Who is my brother?" might sound rather flippant, but to the Jews in the crowd, it would have been quite familiar. "Who is my mother? Who is my brother?" matters because who people are in relationship to you defines your obligations to them. It is a common Jewish practice to pick apart each and every word. What does this really mean? Who is this talking about? "Who is my mother? Who are my brothers?" is a question of great importance.

Traditional Jewish law explicitly dictates certain obligations to one's family of origin. Possibly the most well-known Jewish familial obligation is when a parent, sibling, or child dies, a Jew is *obligated* to say the *Mourner's Kaddish* daily for 11 months. Note the word "obligated" here, because practices around *Kaddish* are changing, but more on that in a moment. There are other family obligations too. The Torah itself contains many explicit *mitzvot* (sacred obligations, often translated as commandments) between parents and their children,[68] including a responsibility to educate your children, honoring your parents, teaching that God is one to your children, and taking care of your parents' physical and economic needs as an adult child. Since the ascendance of rabbinic Judaism after the destruction of the Second Temple in Jerusalem in 70 AD, Jewish status has traditionally been conferred matrilineally: you are Jewish if your mother is Jewish (or if you convert through a formal process). Children from non-Jewish birth parents who are adopted by Jewish parents must technically convert in order to be considered Jewish. For the seeming clarity that traditional Jewish law offers on what family is and who is considered Jewish, there is—and has always been—a blurring of lines there, too.

One of the Jewish people's foundational stories is the Exodus from Egypt, led by Moses, Aaron, and Miriam. It is so important that we tell the story every year during the Passover seder and *Mi*

Chamocha, Moses's "song at the sea," recounting our crossing of the Sea of Reeds out of Egypt is included in the Jewish *siddur*—the collection of daily prayers. In one of the Jewish people's most important, identity-shaping moments, we were blurring boundaries there too. Exodus 12 recounts:[69] "The Israelites journeyed from Rameses to Succoth, about six hundred thousand fighting men on foot, aside from noncombatants. Moreover, a mixed multitude went up with them, and very much livestock, both flocks and herds" (37–38). It was not just Israelites who left Egypt; a "multitude" of other non-Jews threw their lot in with the Israelite people and were integrated into the Israelite community. The traditional requirement to say *Kaddish* is understood to apply only to Jews for their *Jewish immediate family*. Thus, a convert would not be required to say *Kaddish* for their non-Jewish parents. However, there nonetheless exists an ancient tradition of saying *Kaddish* for non-Jews: the earliest recorded instance is in the 12th century in Germany. Many modern communities expect converts to say *Kaddish* for all of their close relatives, Jewish or not. Further still, while not a formal requirement, many Jews expand this practice to include grandparents with whom they are close. LGBTQ+ Jews often say *Kaddish* for members of their chosen family.

Do not be fooled by movies and love songs that say family has to look a certain way: family has *always* been blurry. While there are both secular and religious voices who will call you to turn inward— only your family counts, only take care of your immediate community, only a certain type of person "counts"—there has always been a counter-voice that cuts across religious belief or non-belief: "draw the circle wider," "we are all obligated to one another," "we all count."

It's not just religions that draw boundaries and obligations around family. The legal systems of most countries assign various rights and responsibilities to the people those systems consider family. Important among them are the rights to make medical decisions and to receive automatic and tax-free inheritance. In the midst and aftermath of the AIDS crisis of the 1980s and 1990s, many LGBTQ+ people made legal marriage an urgent priority when it had not previously been. Queer people have long been pioneers of chosen family—creating family-like bonds and networks with people not related by blood but bound together by choice. Queer chosen families are often a sprawling network of best friends, looser acquaintances, good friends of friends of good friends, mentors, lovers, former lovers, and more, but as nearly a generation of gay men fell ill with AIDS and began dying in catastrophic numbers, hospitals didn't much care about decades-long partners or other types of chosen family. In the absence of a legally married spouse, the healthcare system defaulted to the wishes of the family of origin, who were often estranged from their queer adult child. I can imagine a nurse coming into the room of an AIDS patient and saying, much like Jesus's followers did to him, "Your mother and brothers are here to see you." And I can imagine him responding much the same way as Jesus: "Who?! Look around, my mother and brothers are already here."

As non-monogamy gains increasing visibility and acceptance, we are wrestling with many of the same issues that LGBTQ+ people wrestle with: we have a bold, new way of relating that *everyone* could benefit from; why aim for assimilation when transformation would enrich us all? And yet, there are undeniably certain rights and protections that are available *right now* to legally married spouses. Non-monogamous people use all sorts of legal and economic tools to try to form families, including cohabitation agreements, joint house deeds, survivorship agreements, power of attorney, wills, and even limited liability companies. In a world where monogamous people are able to simply sign a marriage license and be considered a family, polyamorous people iron out—at great cost of time, energy, and emotion—exactly who our family is and what family means to us.

This issue of "who is family" and "how is family defined" came into sharp relief nearly a decade after I first began practicing polyamory. My long-term boyfriend and I had been considering both legal marriage and a social wedding-like ceremony when I started dating a new partner. After just a few months, I realized this was going to be a serious relationship and after our relationship continued to blossom over the following months, my other partner and I began to reconsider our marriage plans. Since legal marriage is only available to two individuals, choosing to marry one partner meant choosing *not* to marry the other. I could see a life with *both* of these people and I wanted to be family with both of them. I was unwilling to let the law say that one but not the other was legally valid, and thus that one was more important and even more "real" than the other. The three of us explored some ways that we might, in the future, structure our relationships to try to legally support and protect each other given the limitations of marriage law in the United States. Non-monogamous people have come up with all sorts of creative solutions to take care of each other in the absence of legal marriage rights. Some people draw up extensive housing contracts, others own property together, some use powers of attorney and advanced medical directives, some even form limited companies and use this to pool their resources. Ultimately, nothing protects our relationships as powerfully as legal marriage (and most of them are significantly more expensive than a simple marriage license). This, to me, is a testament to the strength and commitment of non-monogamous relationships. In a world stacked against the way we find, form, and sustain loving relationships, we continue to ask "who is my family?" without taking the answer for granted.

Our current marriage-centric way of building lives and families together does a disservice to more than just polyamorous people. It significantly hampers all sorts of relationships that are family in the deepest sense of the word, such as single dear friends who live and grow old together, blended families who are no longer married but who are nonetheless vitally important to one another, siblings who take care of each other, grandchildren responsible for their grandparents, widows and widowers who form later-in-life relationships but who never remarry, and more.

"Who is my family?" "Who is my partner?" are questions not just with legal ramifications but also with social ones. While our current legal, capitalist, patriarchal society says that it's your nuclear family versus the world, our monogamous-centric culture has a similar refrain: there is your "one and only" and then there is everyone else. In fact, the sexist trope of wives and in-laws always at odds relies on a mononormative premise: your romantic partner trumps everyone else and there is only space for that one person at the center of your life. Any shift in group social dynamics is always bound to include some bumps—even a friend moving away or a new friend joining a group can cause some waves—but the severity of the tension between families of origin and new spouses is often born from competition for "the top spot" in a person's life, a competition that could be replaced entirely if only we'd draw on polyamorous wisdom. A little over a year into our relationship, that same partner went through a gut-wrenching breakup with his other partner. I had a work event that evening and so it was *my* partner, who was not dating him, who went over to his house to be with him. They went out to dinner together and later that night to a performance at the Metropolitan Opera, complete with some late-night ice cream. Whether polyamorous, open, monogamous, or something else entirely, when we expand our notion of "who is my family?" we create space for more love, more support, more connection, more commitment, and more care.

Here too, polyamorous people, who have long practiced expansive ideas of family, have a growing edge when it comes to who we consider family, who we consider partners, and perhaps most importantly, how we relate to those who are neither. The polyamorous community has come up with a brilliant collection of names and descriptors for our various types of partners, the partners of our partners, and other people we are connected to through love and law, as well as all the different ways we relate to one another. Here is a sampling of some of them:

Metamours: A partner of your partner, with whom you are not in a romantic or sexual relationship. The name is a play on the word "paramour," a delightfully juicy word that could connote all types of partners.

Comets: A partner you see infrequently but with some regularity. Like a comet, this type of partner cycles in and out of your life, usually based on geographic constraints but there could be any number of other reasons for the cyclical nature of your relationship, such as the demands of an academic-calendar-based profession.

Primary/Secondary/Tertiary partners: Some non-monogamous people use hierarchical labels to describe the relative importance of their various partners. Sometimes these labels are rigidly enforced and come with attendant power of the partners "below" them, while others use them more loosely to *describe* the priority, time commitment, and emotional entanglement given to various partners without (meaning to) asserting a power dynamic.

Sweethearts/Lovers: Alternative titles to "boyfriend," "girlfriend," and "partner" used by some polyamorous people to describe a relationship that has both emotional and romantic entanglements but does not (or has not yet) risen to the level of a formal commitment.

Nesting partners: This label was specifically created to describe a partner with whom you live (and share attendant home-making commitments with) but with whom you are intentionally not "primary partners" with. Over time, it has also come to be used by some people to describe a primary partner with whom they also live.

Queer platonic partners: A style of relating where partners share deep love for and commitment to each other while being expressly platonic (neither sexual nor romantic). Queer platonic partnerships often share many or most of the other characteristics of long-term romantic and sexual partnerships, including living together, shared finances, emotional support, future planning, and joint decision making.

Kitchen table poly: A style of non-monogamy where all partners and their partners are comfortable spending time together, for example sharing a meal together at a kitchen table. Metamours not only know of each other's existence, they also know about at least some personal details and may (or may not) have their own independent relationships with each other.

Parallel poly: A style of non-monogamy where partners know of each other's existence but whose lives do not ever intersect. Each relationship stays separate from the other.

Garden party poly: A style of non-monogamy that is more interconnected than parallel poly and less intimate than kitchen table poly. Metamours and other members of a polypod know of each other's existence and are comfortable spending casual time together and making small talk, for instance at a garden party, but do not have in-depth relationships or emotional connection with each other.

Partners: Some people prefer simply the word "partner" without any further descriptor to describe their various partners. There's a pragmatic reason for this: it's simpler to just have one single catch-all word for everyone, and there is also a philosophical reason: people might infer varying levels of significance based on the descriptor attached where none is intended. This is one way to keep it simple.

Of course, not all of the people in our lives fit neatly into even these expansive offerings. Like Steven for me, there are some people who have a significance in our lives that goes beyond our current vocabulary. What's the word for "Someone I love dearly and do lots of relationship-like activities with but with whom I have no formal commitments"? Or the word for "We used to just fuck but then we shifted into being friends and stopped having sex for a few years but these days we have sex once every other year or so and also we've known each other for a decade"? Or "She used to be my domme and then my friend and now we are creative collaborators"? Sometimes I bemoan the lack of easily available language to describe many of the closest people in my life, but at the same time, I think part of what makes each of those relationships so holy is precisely this lack of a neat and tidy word for them. The hazy, shifting, liminal quality of them is a space for the divine to break in. As you consider how polyamory might enrich your faith, or how spirituality adds deeper meaning to your relationships, be on the lookout for the people who blur boundaries and defy expectations. You may not be able—or even want—to give them a precise label, but pay attention, take note of them, and remember that they are holy.

If you are monogamous, you can still use the ideas and ideals of polyamory to enrich your life and relationships. Marriage, one of the most-prized life moments in modern Western culture, is often the starting point of tensions between families, as the couple begins to disentangle themselves from their families of origin and form their own, self-contained families. Time becomes split between two competing families. Many people further compartmentalize their lives by keeping their various friend groups separate. There is only so much time and it quickly becomes scarce. But it doesn't have to be that way. Over the past many years, my sister and brother-in-law, inspired by the model of queer and polyamorous love, friendship, and relationships that they have seen in me and my friends and partners, have worked to integrate their families, rather than view them as separate and competing. Each summer, we take a combined family beach vacation; we recently started celebrating Thanksgiving together as one big combined family on the day after Thanksgiving, and my brother-in-law's parents, brother, and brother's girlfriend all came to my wedding. It's the wisdom of kitchen table polyamory applied to a monogamous context: everyone is invited, we are enriched by each other's presence, we don't have to compete. It feels like a sprawling polycule, where many of us are connected through multiple degrees of separation but there is still deep love, affection, and commitment. Who is my sister's husband's brother's wife? Family.

As you consider the people in your life who matter most, it is important to take stock of how easy it is to prioritize family and romantic relationships over platonic ones. This is, unfortunately, true even among polyamorous people. Expansive polycules is one model where polyamorous people set an example for what robust community care can look like. But if our definition of family—and our practices of support, inclusion, and community—is limited only to those we are having sex with (or want to be having sex with!), we are not as expansive or boundary-breaking as we think, and are limiting rather than expanding our imagination of what a diverse definition of the "love" in "polyamory" might look like. Worse still, we run the risk of replicating sexist, racist, ableist, transphobic, fatphobic, and other exclusionary desirability politics in our communities and relationships, further excluding people who are also pushed to the margins of more mainstream support systems. Whether you are monogamous or non-monogamous, the invitation here is to push the response to the question of "Who is family?" toward ever greater inclusion and possibility.

CHAPTER 13

Conclusion: Living Into Love Beyond Monogamy

A popular wedding reading for Jews and Christians of all orientations is from the book of Ruth: "Wherever you go, I will go; and wherever you stay, I will stay. Your people will be my people, and your God will be my God. Wherever you die, I will die, and there I will be buried." It's a beautiful proclamation of love and commitment between two people. Many LGBTQ+ people find it particularly meaningful because it is a commitment between two women: spoken from Ruth to her mother-in-law Naomi. I find it meaningful for another reason: it reminds me of chosen family. For too many people, our relationships have been marked by expectations: expectations of the gender of our partner, expectations of the roles we will play in our relationship, expectations around sex, expectations around chores, expectations around family. This is true whether you come from a religious background or not: the pressure to ride the relationship escalator all the way to the top—to be in a couple, to get married, and to have children—is intense and unrelenting, especially for women. Religious pressures only compound those expectations.

As I hope you've seen throughout this book, there are abundant possibilities for how you structure your life and your faith. God can even be your wingman. Let's close this book back where we began: Adam and Eve. There's more to this archetypal relationship than meets the eye. Genesis 1 and 2 tell two different versions of the creation story. While you may have heard that Genesis 1 has the overview and Genesis 2 has the details, that's a misrepresentation of the text. It's a way to try to make the Bible speak in a unified voice when, as we've seen, the Bible is anything but unified. In Genesis 1, two humans are created together as the final act of creation:

> And God created humankind in the divine image, creating it in the image of God—creating them male and female.

Genesis 2 tells a different story. In Genesis 2, first before there were any clouds or rain, God caused water to spring up from the earth. Then God created the first human, "when no shrub of the field was yet on earth and no grasses of the field had yet sprouted, because God had not sent rain upon the earth and there were no human beings to till the soil." Then, after God created the human, God planted a garden in Eden, and then caused all the other plants to spring up over the earth. After that, God noticed that the human was lonely. "It is not good for the Human to be alone; I will make a fitting counterpart for him." So God became the human's wingman to try to help the human not be so alone. God started creating animals and bringing them to the human as potential mates. "And God formed out of the earth all the wild beasts and all the birds of the sky, and brought them to the Human to see what he would call them; and whatever the Human called each living creature, that would be its name." But every time God brought one to the human, it wasn't quite right. It wasn't until, perhaps exasperated and out of options, God put the Human to sleep and split him in two, creating from him another human. Now there was man and woman, Adam and Eve. It was then that Adam made a proclamation that I didn't fully understand until I fell in love for the first time:

This one at last
Is bone of my bones
And flesh of my flesh.

God had set out to create "a helper that is perfect for him" and here, in Eve, Adam found someone perfect for him. He chose. Choice. Agency. He could have chosen differently. He didn't just take the first option God presented to him. He said, "That was a nice try, God, but you didn't get it quite right. Try again." And God did. God tried again and again and again until God got it right for Adam. It was never God's agenda that he made the human a wife; it was always God's agenda that he helped the human to not be alone.

There are lots of ways to not be alone. Married, monogamous partnership is one of those ways. Even there, though, you will need more than your spouse. A growing volume of research shows that straight men rely on their wife for nearly all of their emotional support and much of their practical, logistical support as well. Acclaimed relationship therapist Esther Perel is often quoted as saying:

> Today, we turn to one person to provide what an entire village once did: a sense of grounding, meaning, and continuity. At the same time, we expect our committed relationships to be romantic as well as emotionally and sexually fulfilling. Is it any wonder that so many relationships crumble under the weight of it all?[70]

Whether you are monogamous, polyamorous, open, monogam-ish, or something else entirely, you can allow the wisdom of polyamory to crack open your expectations and guide you in creating healthier, more robust relationships of all types.

"To be with God," James Baldwin wrote in *Nobody Knows My Name*,[71] "is really to be involved with some enormous, overwhelming desire, and joy, and power which you cannot control, which controls you." In *A Lover's Discourse*, Roland Barth[72] wrote:

The gesture of the amorous embrace seems to fulfill, for a time, the subject's dream of total union with the loved being: The longing for consummation with the other... In this moment, everything is suspended: time, law, prohibition: nothing is exhausted, nothing is wanted: all desires are abolished, for they seem definitively fulfilled.

I hear echoes of the same theme in both: that our relationship with the divine and our relationship with those closest to us are enormous, all-consuming, boundary-breaking, transcendent-touching. To be with God or to be with a lover or to be laughing so hard with a life-long friend that you are gasping for breath or to be at the bedside of a dying best friend is to be in tune with something bigger than yourself. There is a reason so many sacred stories use the language of love in their metaphors for the divine. They are both expansive and all-encompassing.

As we have explored a polyamorous perspective on faith and spirituality over the course of this book, I hope one theme in particular has continued to come up for you: possibilities. Polyamory is full of possibilities and when we apply that wisdom to our faith life, even more possibilities bubble up, enriching all areas of our lives, regardless of our relationship structure. Polyamory is, of course, about the possibility of loving multiple partners, but it also inspires the way we love our metamours, our friends, our neighbors, and our wider community. It's sometimes about the number of partners we have sex with, but it can also transform how we think about sex in general and the value we place on different types of sexual connections. There is a wisdom to be learned from the intentional way that polyamorous people form and keep commitments that would be particularly useful in all sorts of settings: monogamous relationships, faith commitments, the expectations between pastors and parishioners.

In 2020, a polyamorous throuple was featured on HGTV's mega-hit *House Hunters*, bringing non-monogamy into the living rooms of millions of Americans across the country. In 2021, the digital series *Red Table Talk*—hosted by Jada Pinkett Smith, Willow Smith, and Jada's mother, Adrienne Banfield-Norri—featured an episode all about polyamory which has now racked up over five million views. In 2022, TikTok drama became international news when Mormon MomToker Taylor Frankie Paul, who at the time[73] had 3.5 million followers, revealed she and her husband had been swinging with a number of other prominent members of the MomTok community. At QueerTheology.com, I work with people—both LGBTQ+ and straight, cisgender—around the world. I've talked with non-monogamous Jews, Christians, Muslims, and atheists, across denominations and in every corner of the globe. Whether you live in rural Oklahoma, downtown Atlanta, or the suburbs of Sydney, non-monogamy is already in your neighborhood.

There's a story in the Talmud about a potential convert approaching two of the great rabbis—Hillel and Shammai—for insight into the Torah's teaching. The potential convert asked each to tell him all of what the Torah taught while standing on one foot. Hillel took him up on the challenge and answered: "That which is hateful to you do not do to others. All the rest is commentary. Now go and learn" (Shabbat 31A). Jesus in the Gospel accounts has a similar answer about what is important to God. When asked what the "greatest commandment" is, Jesus answers:

> You shall love the Lord your God with all your heart and with all your soul and with all your mind. This is the great and first commandment. And a second is like it: You shall love your neighbor as yourself. On these two commandments depend all the Law and the Prophets.

We see a similar injunction in the Koran (al-Nisaa 4:36) to love both neighbor and stranger:

Serve God, and join not any partners with Him; and do good—to parents, kinsfolk, orphans, those in need, neighbors who are near, neighbors who are strangers, the companion by your side, the way-farer (ye meet), and what your right hands possess.

One of the central teachings in Hinduism, Buddhism, and Jainism is *ahimsa*. While the word is often translated as "non-violence," it is really a sweeping concept about the interconnectedness of everything and our sacred responsibility to do no harm—and to interrupt the cycles and machinations of harm in our world. Jews have been asking the questions, "Who is my neighbor? And what is my responsibility toward them?" for over 3,000 years. Polyamorous communities are asking similar questions, though sometimes we ask, "Who is my metamour and what is my responsibility toward them?" instead of, "Who is my neighbor?" There are many points of difference among the world's religions but taking care of those around you is central to them all, at least in theory if not always in practice.

The practice of polyamory has profoundly shaped my life. It is intertwined with and inseparable from both my queerness and my faith. In Judaism, the Shema is one of the central prayers of our faith. It acknowledges the oneness of God. That intertwining of your sexual orientation, your gender, your relationship style, and all other aspects and experiences of yourself, like your ethnicity, immigration status, family makeup, and more—all of that is wound up together with God. And so it is also for your friends, family, and neighbors. My hope for you is that no matter your relationship structure, these insights from polyamory will become bound up in you too and will enrich your spirituality and your sexuality. May you see in yourself and in all the ways that you love, reflections of the divine. It is all already holy.

Endnotes

1   Covey, S. (1989). *The 7 Habits of Highly Effective People*. New York, Simon and Schuster.

2   Lehmiller, J.J. (2020). Fantasies about consensual nonmonogamy among persons in monogamous romantic relationships. *Archives of Sexual Behavior*, 49, 2799–2812. https://doi.org/10.1007/s10508-020-01788-7

3   Her. (2018, November 24). *Science says this is how many dates you have to go on before you find 'The One'*. https://her.ie/life/whats-your-number-study-finds-the-average-number-of-dates-and-relationships-before-we-find-the-one-903300

4   Brody, J.E. (2018, January 22). When a partner cheats. *The New York Times*. www.nytimes.com/2018/01/22/well/marriage-cheating-infidelity.html

5   Jason Silva: Shots of Awe. (2015, May 19). *Why Do We Fall In Love?* [Video]. YouTube. www.youtube.com/watch?v=_rJKWh4ixAo

6   Jason Silva: Shots of Awe. (2015, October 27). *The Sad Tragic Truth About Our Relationships* [Video]. YouTube. www.youtube.com/watch?v=_t2xdJhlM8Y

7   Cox, D.A. (2021) *The State of American Friendship: Change, Challenges, and Loss.* Survey Center of American Life. www.americansurveycenter.org/research/the-state-of-american-friendship-change-challenges- and-loss

8   Haupert, M.L. *et al.* (2016). Prevalence of experiences with consensual nonmonogamous relationships: Findings from two national samples of single Americans. *Journal of Sex & Marital Therapy*, 43(5), 424–440.

9   YouGov. (2020). One-third of Americans say their ideal relationship is non-monogamous. https://today.yougov.com/society/articles/27639-millennials-monogamy-poly-poll-survey-data

10 hooks, b. (2018). *All About Love: New Visions*. New York: HarperCollins.

11 www.cdc.gov/nchs/fastats/unmarried-childbearing.htm

12 Wright, C. (2012). *Breakup Parties*. Exile Lifestyle. https://exilelifestyle.com/breakup-parties

13 Murphy, B.G. & Kearns, S.T.L. (Hosts). (2024, July 28). Holding Space with Avra Shapiro (No. 549) [Audio podcast episode]. In *Queer Theology*. QueerTheology.com. www.queertheology.com/podcast/549

14 Pew Research Centre. (2017). Many countries favor specific religions, officially or unofficially. www.pewresearch.org/religion/2017/10/03/many-countries-favor-specific-religions-officially-or-unofficially

15 Shen, P. (Director). (2003). *Flight from Death: The Quest for Immortality* [Film]. Transcendental Media.

16 Wilson, R.A. (1962). Sexual freedom: Why is it feared? *Mattachette Review*, 8(8). https://rawilsonfans.org/sexual-freedom

17 Newport, C. (2019). *Digital Minimalism: Choosing a Focused Life in a Noisy World*. New York: Portfolio/Penguin.

18 Jason Silva: Shots of Awe. (2019, February 22). *What Is the Sacred?* [Video]. YouTube. www.youtube.com/watch?v=yFQ92U_c-BE

19 Solomon, S. (2015). *The Worm at the Core: On the Role of Death in Life*. New York: Random House.

20 Jason Silva: Shots of Awe. (2019, February 22). *What is the Sacred?* [Video]. YouTube. www.youtube.com/watch?v=yFQ92U_c-BE

21 Heschel, A.J. (1997). *God in Search of Man: A Philosophy of Judaism* (p.45). New York: Farrar, Straus and Giroux.

22 Easton, D. & Hardy, J. (1997). *The Ethical Slut: A Guide to Infinite Sexual Possibilities*. Berkeley, CA: Greenery Press.

23 Armstrong, K. (1900). *The Lost Art of Scripture: Rescuing Sacred Texts* (p.21). New York: Alfred Knopf.

24 Armstrong, K. (1900). *The Lost Art of Scripture: Rescuing Sacred Texts* (p.787, Kindle). New York: Alfred Knopf.

25 Anonymous. (1990). *Queers Read This*. www.qrd.org/qrd/misc/text/queers.read.this

26 @noahwaybabes https://twitter.com/noahwaybabes/status/1759462027704345015

27 Personal interview with Jonah Wheeler, September 16, 2024.

28 Tolentino, C. (2024). *Native American Gods and Goddesses: Deities from Different Cultures*. History Cooperative.

29 Al-Kadhi, A. (2020). The Queer Prophet. In R. Hunt (ed.) *The Book of Queer Prophets* (p.7). London: William Collins.

30 Heschel, A.J. (1983/2022). *I Asked for Wonder: A Spiritual Anthology* (ed. Samuel H. Dresner, p.21). New York: Crossroad Publishing.

31 My Jewish Learning. *Pirkei Avot: Ethics of the Fathers, Chapter 5*. www.myjewishlearning.com/article/pirkei-avot-ethics-of-the-fathers-chapter-5

32 Plaskow, J. (1990). *Standing Again at Sinai*. San Francisco, CA: Harper and Row.

33 Jason Silva: Shots Of Awe. (2014, March 11). *Love is the Greatest Pain* [Video]. YouTube. www.youtube.com/watch?v=fYwrkzNtlgI

34 About Islam. (2019, January 26). *Explaining God's Love in the Quran*. https://aboutislam.net/reading-islam/understanding-islam/explaining-gods-love-in-the-quran

35 Miller, M. (n.d.). *Chesed, Gevura, & Tiferet: Harmonizing kindness and strength*. Chabad-Lubavitch Media Center. www.chabad.org/kabbalah/article_cdo/aid/380796/jewish/Chesed-Gevura-Tiferet.htm

36 Psychology Today. *Limerence*. www.psychologytoday.com/us/basics/limerence

37 Arnold, T. (2024). *Mother Teresa's 'spiritual darkness' was not depression or loss of faith, scholar explains*. EWTN. https://ewtn.co.uk/article-mother-teresas-spiritual-darkness-was-not-depression-or-loss-of-faith-scholar-explains

38 Fern, J. (2023). *Polywise: A Deeper Dive into Navigating Open Relationships* (p.32). Vancouver Island: Thornapple Press.

39 Coffey, C. & Crozier, M. (Hosts). (2022, January 4). Brian G. Murphy of QueerTheology.com. Finding the Divine in Queerness and Polyamory (No. 32) [Audio podcast episode]. In *Thereafter*. https://podcasters.spotify.com/pod/show/thereafter/episodes/032---Brian-G--Murphy-of-QueerTheology-com--Finding-The-Divine-in-Queerness-and-Polyamory-e1cg00a)

40 Witherspoon, R.G. & Theodore, P.S. (2021). Exploring minority stress and resilience in a polyamorous sample. *Archives of Sexual Behavior*, 50(4), 1367–1388. https://doi.org/10.1007/s10508-021-01995-w

41 *Holy Bible, New International Version*. (2011/1973). Micah 6:8. Biblica. 9:26

42 *New King James Version Bible*. (1982). James 2:20

43 Shanker, D. (2023, April 20). *New Data Shows US Food Waste Is Getting Worse*. Bloomberg. www.bloomberg.com/news/articles/2023-04-20/the-us-has-a-food-waste-problem-and-it-s-getting-worse?embedded-checkout=true

44 Rainn. *What Consent Looks Like*. https://rainn.org/articles/what-is-consent

45 Lindgren, J., Matlack, E. & Winston, D. (Hosts). (2019, July 2). Rules vs. Agreements feat. Boundaries (No. 227) [Audio podcast episode]. In *Multiamory*. www.multiamory.com/podcast/227-rule-vs-agreements

46 Tillich, Paul. Dynamics of Faith. HarperCollins, 1957. https://utppublishing.com/doi/pdf/10.3138/uram.16.1-2.149

47 Mahtani, N. (2022, May 21). *Here's what it means to DTR, according to a clinical psychologist*. Women's Health. www.womenshealthmag.com/relationships/a40012060/dtr-meaning

48 Chodron, P. (2022). *How We Live Is How We Die* (p.6). Boulder, CO: Shambhala.

49 Rhee, H. (2005). *Early Christian Literature*. London: Routledge. https://doi.org/10.4324/9780203001547

50 www.polycocktails.com

51 Aggie Sez. (2012, November 29). *Riding the Relationship Escalator (or Not)*. Solo Poly. https://solopoly.net/2012/11/29/riding-the-relationship-escalator-or-not

52 Fern, J. (2023). *Polywise: A Deeper Dive into Navigating Open Relationships*. Vancouver Island: Thornapple Press.

53 *THE JPS TANAKH: Gender-Sensitive Edition*. (2023). (Stein, D.E.S. (Trans.)). The Jewish Publication Society.

54 https://www.cityharvest.org/hunger-in-nyc

55 Personal conversation/interview (September 19, 2024).

56 Bell, A.P. & Weinberg, M.S. (1978). *Homosexualities: A Study of Diversity Among Men and Women*. New York: Simon and Schuster. https://archive.org/details/homosexualitiessbellrich/page/134/mode/2up

57 Wilder, T. (2020, May 31). *Candy Marcum, a therapist and lesbian, has helped gay men in Texas since the early days of AIDS*. The Body. www.thebody.com/article/candy-marcum-therapist-since-aids-early-days

58 The Hindu Portal. (2015). Hospitality in Hindu Culture. www.thehinduportal.com/2015/12/hospitality-in-hindu-culture.html

59 Chodron, P. (2021, March 20). *Nothing to (Im)prove*. Tricycle: The Buddhist Review. https://tricycle.org/article/pema-chodron-lovingkindness

60 Cox, D. (2021, June 8). *The state of American friendship: Change, challenges, and loss*. Survey Center on American Life. www.americansurveycenter.org/research/the-state-of-american-friendship-change-challenges-and-loss

61 Personal communication with Zach Bloom, Manager of Business Planning and Initiatives in the Office of Sustainability at the Port Authority of NY & NJ, a project manager with a decade of transit industry experience in New York.

62 Abrams, Z. (2023). The science of why friendships keep us healthy. *Monitor of Psychology*, 54(4), 42. www.apa.org/monitor/2023/06/cover-story-science-friendship

63 Jacobs, J. (1961). *The Death and Life of Great American Cities*. New York: Random House.

64 Witherspoon, R.G. & Theodore, P.S. (2021). Exploring minority stress and resilience in a polyamorous sample. *Archives of Sexual Behavior*, 50(4), 1367–1388. https://doi.org/10.1007/s10508-021-01995-w

65 Heschel, A.J. (1976). *Man Is Not Alone: A Philosophy of Religion* (p.20). New York: Farrar, Straus and Giroux.

66 Frishman, E. (2007). *Mishkan T'filah: A Reform Siddur: Complete: Shabbat, Weekdays, and Festivals* (Transliterated) (p.32).

67 L'Engle, M. (1980). *Walking on Water: Reflections on Faith and Art* (p.42). Wheaton, IL: H. Shaw.

68 My Jewish Learning.(n.d.). *Jewish parent/child relationships*. www.myjewishlearning.com/article/jewish-parentchild-relationships

69 *The Contemporary Torah*. (Stein, D.E.S. (Trans.)). (2006). The Jewish Publication Society.

70 Perel, E. (2006). *Mating in Captivity: Reconciling the Erotic and the Domestic* (p.xiv). New York: HarperCollins.

71 DeCort, A.J. (2022). *Many Many Colours: The Ethical Vision of James Baldwin*. Andrew DeCort. https://andrew-decort.com/essays/many-many-colors-the-ethical-vision-of-james-baldwin

72 Barth, R. (1978). *A Lover's Discourse*. New York: Hill and Wang.

73 Cohen, D. & Truffant-Wong, O. (2024). *A refresher on the Mormon MomTok Drama*. The Cut. www.thecut.com/2024/09/mormon-momtok-swingers-drama-explained.html

of related interest

The Anxious Person's Guide to Non-Monogamy
Your Guide to Open Relationships,
Polyamory and Letting Go
Lola Phoenix
Foreword by Kathy G. Slaughter
ISBN 978 1 83997 2 133
eISBN 978 1 83997 2 140

Expansive Love
A Practical Guide to Relationship Anarchy
Tuck Malloy
ISBN 978 1 80501 1 316
eISBN 978 1 80501 1 309

Monogamy? In This Economy?
Finances, Childrearing, and Other
Practical Concerns of Polyamory
Laura Boyle
ISBN 978 1 80501 1 187
eISBN 978 1 80501 1 194

The Non-Monogamy Journal
90+ Scenarios and Questions to Define Boundaries
and Make Polyamory Work for You
Lola Phoenix
ISBN 978 1 80501 4 225
eISBN 978 1 80501 4 232